CODE BLUE

Steve and Juanito

Love you both

12-25-95

[signature]

CODE BLUE

Urgent Care for the American Youth Emergency

Nicky Cruz

VINE
BOOKS

Servant Publications
Ann Arbor, Michigan

Vine Books is an imprint of Servant Publications especially designed to serve Evangelical Christians.

All scripture quotations, unless otherwise indicated, are taken from the HOLY BIBLE, NEW INTERNATIONAL VERSION®. © 1973, 1978, 1984 by International Bible Society. Used by permission of Zondervan Publishing House. All rights reserved.

The "NIV" and "New International Version" trademarks are registered in the United States Patent and Trademark Office by International Bible Society. Use of either trademark requires the permission of International Bible Society.

Excerpts from Bill Bennett's speech, "What Really Ails America," that appear in the appendix are used by permission of the author.

All names and identifying details contained in these stories have been changed to protect the privacy of those involved.

Published by Servant Publications
P.O. Box 8617
Ann Arbor, Michigan 48107

Cover design by Multnomah Graphics
Cover photo, cracked window image: Laubacher/Photogroup 1989. Used by permission. Cover photo, chalk outline image: Ron Chapple 1993. Used by permission.

95 96 97 98 99 10 9 8 7 6 5 4 3 2 1

Printed in the United States of America
ISBN 0-89283-904-X

Library of Congress Cataloging-in-Publication Data

Cruz, Nicky.
    Code blue : urgent care for the American youth emergency /
Nicky Cruz.
        p.   cm.
    Includes bibliographical references.
    ISBN 0-89283-904-X
    1. Problem youth—Rehabilitation—United States.   2.
Juvenile delinquency—United States—Prevention.   3. Youth—
Religious life—United States.   4. Salvation.   I. Title.
HV1431.C78   1995
362.7'4'0973—dc20   95-19395
                                                              CIP

DEDICATION

I dedicate this book to special people that have deeply touched my life in one of my greatest times of need.

Dr. Jim Caldwell, a most faithful friend and board member who has been closer than a brother. He and his wife, Joyce, have always been there for me when I needed them.

Mr. Jim DeVries and his wife, Judy, who have also always been there for me when I needed them. I am happy to say that this man's wealth has abounded to many, and his generosity will not be forgotten by me.

Dr. David Greenberg, my cardiologist, whose words God guided. He was also an encouragement to me.

Dr. Jerome Bramschreiber, my personal physician who has attended me and my family throughout the years.

Dr. Allen Bettis for his counseling and wise advice.

SPECIAL THANKS

Thanks first and foremost to my precious family. They are a special hedge that God has put around me. That's what a family is all about—a circle of love and forbearance.

Patrick and Alicia Dow, my right hand and left hand. For sure they sustained my tired arms many times. They came to Nicky Cruz Outreach at God's appointed time. God is always on time. Alicia, especially, provided invaluable insight, research, and feedback on this particular project.

Contents

INTRODUCTION

Code Blue in Monterrey

A few years ago I received an invitation to visit some good friends in Monterrey, Mexico. They are wonderful Christian people, richly gifted in hospitality, who often open their home to friends desperately in need of a break from the rat race. That description definitely fit me the day they asked if we might like to spend some relaxed time with them. I had just finished one crusade and had only a few days before the next one was to begin, so I was exhausted. I accepted their invitation immediately—not only because I needed the rest, but because they had become like family to me.

I quickly got a few things together and headed south to bask for a while in the welcome heat of the Mexican sun. A native Puerto Rican like me knows how to appreciate blue skies and balmy temperatures. But before too many days had passed, I began to feel... odd. I had developed a cyst on my left elbow, and each movement of my arm sent fiery bolts of pain screaming through my body. I didn't think it was quite an emergency, but I did want to get it checked out.

Fortunately, my friends knew someone who was studying to become a doctor. This man was a young Christian and very excited about Jesus. He was from a very rich, prominent Arab family in Monterrey and was doing an internship required by his university in order to be certified as a full-fledged doctor.

My friends introduced me to this young man and we hit it off immediately. When he learned that I was having some discomfort, he said, "Nicky, let's go to the hospital. I have some friends who work in the emergency room; I can get them to see you." Even though I had known him only a short time, I trusted him. He seemed to know what he was talking about—and I was in pain. My arm had swelled up alarmingly. So we decided to go.

It was midnight by the time we arrived at the hospital. I suppose I had an image in mind of a clean, efficient, disinfected, and orderly American hospital. But that's not what greeted my astonished eyes. In fact, I was in for the shock of my life.

Wherever I looked, there were people. People in line. People in chairs. People on the floor. People moaning in pain or screaming in agony. People crazy with fear or people passed out from their injuries. People, people, people—and all of them with problems greater than my own.

The place was packed to the rafters. What doctors there were scurried about from patient to patient, urgently trying to determine who needed the most immediate attention. But there just weren't enough doctors to see to all the patients—not even with the students who had been called in to lend a hand.

I took one unbelieving look at the bedlam erupting all over the emergency room, turned to my new friend and whispered, "I think I need to go to the bathroom."

He quickly obliged my request and escorted me to a part of the hospital that resembled a dormitory. The space had been set aside for the exclusive use of doctors and students. When I opened the door to the bathroom I got my second shock of the evening.

Scattered about on makeshift cots—like bums on Skid Row— were six or seven exhausted doctors, vainly trying to sneak in a couple of hours of sleep after working around the clock in the emergency room. My presence in the room went completely unnoticed.

A few moments later I was taken to another room in the hospital. Again, I simply couldn't believe what I saw. Three people died right in front of me. One lady had been in a horrible car accident; her body was now one indistinguishable mass of exposed, broken bones, mangled flesh, and blood. A man, perhaps involved in the same crash, was waiting to have a bottle removed from where it had embedded itself in his body. Blood covered the room—in pools on the floor, smeared on the walls, and even spattered on the ceiling. Wherever I looked, there was blood.

As I looked at all the carnage, I couldn't help but ask myself, *What am I doing here?* By this time I had pretty much forgotten why I had come in the first place.

Without a doubt, it was the most frightening scene I have ever witnessed. I thought I was back in Brooklyn in the midst of a rumble, with bodies falling everywhere. There was a war on, and the casualties were mounting out of control. At least, that's what it felt like to me.

Obviously, it left a lasting impression in my mind. It would even be true to say that the bloody scene damaged me psychologically for a while. I felt so overwhelmingly sad for the people. I thought, *Father, I rejoice in the privilege we have in the United States—but I have never seen anything like this in my life.*

At least, I'd never seen anything like it until now.

CODE BLUE IN AMERICA

The American Medical Association in 1989 formed a national commission charged with evaluating America's youth. The commission concluded that our youth are in a state of "national emergency" and that we are facing an "unprecedented adolescent crisis." The commission titled its report *Code Blue*, a term many hospitals use to refer to a patient in critical condition who has stopped breathing and whose vital signs have gone flat. In other words—get this patient breathing, or call the coroner.

I'm convinced the AMA got it exactly right. Our youth are in critical condition, they've just about stopped breathing, and their vitals are threatening to go flat. We have to do something, *now*, or we might as well call the coroner.

Except there won't be any coroner to call, because our nation itself will be dead.

Please don't think I'm being overly dramatic. I'm not. I've been with street kids in Los Angeles. I've talked with "gangstas" in New York. I've listened to hurting kids in Texas, in Arkansas, in Colorado, in Illinois, and all across this nation, and what I'm hearing and seeing is breaking my heart.

The youth of this nation aren't merely "at risk," they're one step away from Code Blue.

And I'm not talking only about kids in the inner cities. The problems we too easily limit to the ghetto and the barrio have rapidly spread to include the suburbs and even rural communities. The Youth Emergency—because that is what it is—has exploded to include all our youth. It's not an inner-city problem anymore (if it ever was).

I haven't made any recent visits to emergency rooms in the United States as I did to the one in Monterrey, but I've definitely seen comparable carnage. Never in my many years of ministry—and not even when I was the leader of the Mau Maus in New York City before I was saved over thirty years ago—have I witnessed more bloody slaughter than is now taking place among the youth of America.

The youth of America are dying, and we seem incapable of stopping it. You don't have to look far to see the urgent nature of this emergency:

- Skyrocketing juvenile crime rates
- Record-breaking jumps in juvenile mortality rates
- Rising gang violence, even in the suburbs
- Polls and music that show a preoccupation with death

Scores of other statistical categories could be mentioned (and many will be later in the book), but for now let me say this: This book is an attempt not only to draw attention to the crisis facing our youth, but to suggest some workable *answers*. It is not enough to tell tragic stories about wasted youth, to wring our hands and curse the darkness. It isn't enough to complain about what is being offered to us "on the menu"; we have been called by the Master himself to go into the steaming kitchen where the heat and the fire are, and help fix the dinner. Jesus said:

> But if the salt loses its saltiness, how can it be made salty again? It is no longer good for anything, except to be thrown out and trampled by men.   **Matthew 5:13**

The apostle Paul must have understood these marching orders, because his own instructions to the young pastor Timothy sounded like this:

> Preach the Word; be prepared in season and out of season; correct, rebuke and encourage—with great patience and careful instruction.... Keep your head in all situations, endure hardship, do the work of an evangelist, discharge all the duties of your ministry.   **2 Timothy 4:2, 5**

The Lord has written those words to us as well; they are our marching orders. *Code Blue* is filled with dramatic stories of a disintegrating youth culture, but it's also filled with hope. Now is not the time to give up! The church is called to be a Holy Ghost Hospital, and we have patients to attend to—patients referred to us by the Savior himself. We need to embrace the conviction that salt is valuable only if the savor is strong and being used as it was intended.

We need to remember at this crucial time that emergency room personnel don't give up when they hear a code blue—they redouble their efforts and fight like madmen for wounded lives. They don't call for the coroner until they've done everything in their power to save a life. There may be blood on the floors, on the walls, and even on the ceilings, but if the patient's heartbeat can be restored, that is all that matters. A life is at stake, hanging in the balance, and every struggle is worth the effort. "Endure hardship... like a good soldier of Christ Jesus" (2 Tm 2:3).

This book was written to encourage us, the body of Christ, to make the effort. I am constantly asked by the gangs: "Where's the difference? How are you different? Show me!" That's a challenge we *must* answer.

THE CAT AND THE BIRD

Before we meet some of the casualties of the American youth crisis and before we consider some possible answers, let me tell you a little fable. It has a lot to say to those of us who have been made a part of the body of Christ.

Once there was a big cat and a little bird who lived in the same house. The cat was forever plotting evil ways to catch the bird and eat him, but the bird was far too quick for him. None of his plans ever worked.

But one day, the cat had an idea. *Perhaps I've been going about this the wrong way,* he thought. *Maybe I don't have to work so hard after all.* And then a devious plan began forming in his mind.

One early morning when the dew was still on the grass and the window was still moist, the cat approached the bird—from a distance—with a proposition.

"Excuse me, friend," said the cat. "I know we haven't always been on the best of terms, but I'm hoping to change all that. You see, I've really fallen in love with the way you look. You're so beautiful! I can't help but admire all your lovely feathers. We cats have only this fur—nothing like your gorgeous feathers."

"Why… thank you," replied the little bird. "But I think I'll stay up here, if it's all the same to you."

"Oh, of course, of course," said the fat cat. "But I wonder— would you be open to a little deal? I'd really love for you to change your mind about me, and I think this deal would change our relationship."

"Go ahead—I'm listening," said the little bird, nervously.

"Here's my proposition," replied the cat. "If you give me one of your beautiful feathers each day—just one, they are so beautiful, and, after all, you have so many—then I'll spare you from having to find your own dinner. You give me one of your gorgeous feathers, and I'll give you the most delicious worms you can imagine. Deal?"

The little bird didn't have to think twice (he really hated having to find his own worms). "Deal!" he chirped happily.

So the next day, the cat did as he promised. He dug up some delicious worms, and the bird gave him a beautiful feather. This went on for many days. The bird relaxed all day long. The cat did all the hard work while the bird basked in the sunshine, sipping a margarita.

One day the little bird looked in a mirror and noticed he was down to his last feather. But since he was hungry, he prepared to pluck it out and hand it over to the cat. But when his feline benefactor arrived, he brought no worms.

"What's the deal?" demanded the bird.

"No deal today!" shouted the cat, as in a flash he pounced on the almost naked bird, wrung his chubby neck, and gobbled him down.

The moral of the story? This is what compromise is like—you give up one feather at a time, until you've lost everything. And too many of us in the church have been playing this feather game for too long.

We think that we can touch sin and compromise ourselves without being tainted. The bird was a fool. He thought that he could be a friend with the cat. Just like the cat and the bird, Christians can never be a friend of the world. Neither can we play with fire and not get burned. We can't compromise without losing that which makes us beautiful and unique (and which keeps us safe!).

Just like the bird, too many of our kids think that they can fool around with things their parents and grandparents have warned them against. Many of today's youth believe they can get away with murder and that nothing will ever hurt them. They think they can play with drugs, witchcraft, sex, gangs, and violence without having to pay a price. But they forget the cat and bird have never gotten along; nothing will ever change in their natures. I'm referring to the cat that's in the world and sometimes inside of us. Wherever the cat appears, he still must be fought. The cat will always eat the bird if the bird isn't careful.

Unfortunately, compromise isn't a problem only for our kids. Too many of us have bought into the liberal and lawless spirit of our age. Slowly we have been duped into believing that we can play with things that always have been wrong. We think we are high-tech, sophisticated, and advanced, but really we are naive and gullible. We are much more accepting than ever before. We embrace everyone under the banner of humanity, and we think that we can accept everyone's beliefs and philosophies. But we cannot. We do need to love and respond to people with compassion, but not at the expense of sacrificing a true, holy commitment to the cause—living a life that is pleasing in God's eyes. If we continue to ignore the danger of compromise, it will slowly creep up on us, pounce, and eat us alive.

We can't afford to do that in the church. We are called to make a difference in our world, to reach out to those who are lost and living in hopelessness. And the youth of our country certainly fit that description.

My passion as an evangelist and my heart as a father both urge me to plead for the church to act *now* to help save our youth. We cannot afford to be casual or to compromise. We have already given away too many feathers; we have listened too long to the cat, and he is about to pounce on our most precious possession, our kids and the next generation.

Code Blue is an urgent call to action. It is a trumpet blast to the church to wake up out of a deep slumber. And it is a father's cry to do whatever we can to save our children. They can be saved. We have both the resources and the mandate to act effectively. The Savior calls us to arms.

Let's outwit the devil. Let's not give away any more feathers. Or any more of our kids.

CHAPTER 1

An Ordinary Friday on Main Street, USA

In the past few years I have been spending more and more of my time in the hurting cities of America. My heart is increasingly burdened for the youth of this nation, boys and girls who are growing up in violent neighborhoods where they expect life to be brutish, nasty, and short.

For the first few days of November 1994, I visited some good friends in South Central Los Angeles. South Central is the area of L.A. hit hard by riots in 1992. Whole blocks were burned to the ground and remain desolate to this day.

I was in South Central to collect information for this book and was invited to tour some of the infamous housing projects in the area, hosted by leaders of Victory Outreach (a fabulous ministry you'll be hearing more about later in the book). It was growing dark, and my hosts kept muttering to themselves, "I can't believe we haven't heard any gunfire yet. What time is it?"

After several such expressions of surprise, the question was only natural: "Why do you expect to hear gunfire on this particular night? What's happening?"

"People just got their checks, and many of them are spending it on alcohol," came the reply. "Then they go out and shoot off their guns. But I can't figure out why we haven't heard any shots yet."

About 7 P.M. as the van was leaving the projects and heading for the freeway, five police cars came squealing over to the curb and stopped, red and blue lights flashing and police officers emerging warily from their vehicles with guns drawn. Another six patrol cars on the left were just yards away, rushing to the scene.

"Oh. There they are," our host said without surprise.

Did you catch what I said? *Without surprise.* What has happened to this country? What has taken us to the place where it is the *absence*—not the presence—of gunfire that surprises us?

"Well, Nicky," someone might be tempted to say, "I appreciate your concern for our country, but don't you think you're overdoing it a bit? After all, you were in South Central L.A.—what did you expect? It's not like the whole country is under siege. In the ghettos, sure. But I live in the suburbs. It's not really a problem where I live."

Oh, really? I wouldn't be too sure if I were you. Especially if you ever go to the movies.

OUT OF NOWHERE

Tim Hawley and his fiancée, Tanea Whittaker, had just left the Lloyd Center shopping mall theater after seeing the Jean Claude Van Damme movie *Hard Target*. It was about 10 P.M. on Friday, September 11, 1993, and they were waiting for Tanea's mother to pick them up near the main entrance of one of the center's anchor department stores. They were due to be married in about a month, and both twenty-two-year-olds were anxious for the day to arrive.

Suddenly a mob of teenagers charged them from a park across the street. "Hang on to your purse!" Tim shouted to Tanea. "We've got to get back inside the mall!"

They never made it.

Before Tim and Tanea could react, one of the youths overtook Tim and started shouting obscenities at him. "Run!" Tim yelled to Tanea, who darted back to the store's entrance and began pounding on the door. "Let me in!" she screamed, but the only person left in the mall, a floor sweeper, ignored her.

When Tanea turned around, she thought she saw two youths attacking Tim from different directions, one carrying a clublike object wrapped in green cloth. The pair tackled Hawley and began kicking him repeatedly in the face and ribs.

Tanea began banging on the door once more, and when she turned around a second time, she saw her fiancé's five-foot-eight, 165-pound body sailing through the air. The angry youths had thrown him down a flight of concrete stairs. Tanea ran to Tim as he began convulsing at her feet.

"My God!" Tanea screamed to no one in particular. "Call the police!"

The attackers, apparently believing they had killed Tim, fled the scene. Police arrived just a few moments after the youths had vanished into the night.[1]

PERMANENT DAMAGE

The attack lasted less than a minute, but Tim was beaten so severely that by the next day he still needed the help of a respirator to breathe. He was immediately taken to an intensive care unit and was attached to a device that monitored the growing pressure in his skull. He drifted in and out of consciousness and was unable to talk for two and a half days. It wasn't until Wednesday of the following week that he could even recall going to the movie.

Tim was diagnosed with blood clots and damage to the frontal lobe of his brain, injuries which required major surgery. Much of the damage was permanent. Since Tim had no medical insurance, city residents who read about his plight in the local newspaper began donating funds to help pay for his medical care. While the support was gratifying, the $4,100 raised wasn't nearly enough to cover Tim's astronomical expenses.[2]

Suddenly, everyone in the city seemed to be asking everybody else: Why did this happen? How could this happen? What had gone wrong?

An investigation eventually determined that Tim had been mauled by three teenagers who were part of a much larger group that had been turned away from a local high school dance earlier that evening. The dance had begun at 8 P.M. at Benson High School, a few blocks from the Lloyd Center. Nineteen parents, staff, administrators, and community members had agreed to supervise the two hundred teens admitted to the dance.

But shortly after 9 P.M., Benson Vice Principal Fred Jackson called school police Lieutenant Steve Hollingsworth to complain about forty to fifty "unwanted" students milling around outside. Hollingsworth was the first officer on the scene, but as the crowd grew and became more and more unruly, four school police officers and another forty city police officers eventually responded. The three youths who later attacked Tim Hawley were among a mob of

---

Where's the Gunfire?

James Fox, a criminologist at Northeastern University, has noted that juvenile homicide is spiraling—since 1984, the number of kids killed has quadrupled. "The flood of the epidemic is with guns," he says.[51]

Gunfire and gangs go together like peanut butter and jelly. Where you have one, you have the other.

According to *Gangs: The Epidemic Sweeping America*, a handbook commissioned by the Colorado Springs Public Safety Association, many gangs are making great efforts to expand beyond their local cities. The handbook claims gangs have taken over about 125 cities throughout the United States, including Salt Lake City, Utah; Fort Wayne, Indiana; and even smaller towns such as Martinsburg, West Virginia.[52]

The handbook says gangs often send one member to another city to "test the waters" to see if the area would be a good location for that particular gang. These scouts find out if there is a market for illegal narcotics, test the limits of any gang prevention programs, and try to recruit other young people.

Shreveport, Louisiana, is one example of this tactic. When a gang called the Rolling 60s sent a member to live with a relative, the area quickly was inundated with drive-by shootings. Drug activity skyrocketed and gang graffiti soon covered formerly pristine homes and businesses. "Shreveport, it seemed, passed the gang litmus test," the handbook concluded.[53]

up to 150 students who were turned away from the dance.[3]

Two weeks after the brutal attack, police arrested Nathaniel Sharay Wilson, Nathaniel Gene Martin, and Michael Enoch Chiles.

Wilson was charged with attempted murder, first-degree assault, intimidation, and a probation violation. Court records showed he was on probation for rape, other sexual charges, and driving a stolen car.

Martin was charged with attempted murder, first-degree assault, and intimidation. He also was charged with fourth-degree assault and second-degree intimidation for punching a forty-two-year-old who was sitting in his car on another side of the shopping center prior to the Hawley beating. Martin had been arrested the previous year for assault and stealing a car.

Chiles was charged with attempted murder, first-degree assault, and intimidation. He admitted kicking Hawley in the head "possibly as many as six to seven times."

George Weatheroy, Jr., a public school police officer, said that all three youths were gang-affected, although none was listed as a gang affiliate. He also said many gang members were at the scene of the attack.

"Gang members always feel that they have to show how tough they are," Weatheroy said.[4]

While Wilson and Martin were eventually prosecuted in juvenile court, Chiles was remanded to adult court.

And the ages of the attackers? Martin was sixteen at the time of the attack, while both Wilson and Chiles were fifteen.[5]

DEATH IN THE CITY

Horrifying, you say? You're right. But let me tell you another story. Just one month before the Hawley beating, thirty-two-year-old Bible school student Dan Cripps was driving home about 10:20 P.M. after weeding the strawberry patch of an elderly member of his church. Dan worked as a groundskeeper at the Bible school, was known as a good athlete, played both guitar and piano, and composed contemporary Christian music. He also served as a counselor to his church's youth groups. With him in the car that evening were his wife, Margaret, and their four-year-old son, Isaiah. Dan was traveling westbound on Glisan Street in stop-and-go traffic when a carload of teens passed him, yelling obscenities at his son.

Dan was indignant and demanded an apology. Instead, a drunken Jose "Paco" Miranda leapt out of his car and punched Dan, who then bounded from his own car and tackled Miranda. The two rolled around on the pavement before Dan, a weight lifter, released the other man. "Get up and leave," Dan said. "This isn't worth it."

Just then, Miranda's friends pulled their car alongside the Cripps' family vehicle. The driver, sixteen-year-old Sothsay Pathoumsat, aimed a gun directly at Dan's stomach and fired a single shot. "This will teach you a lesson," he said.

Miranda then jumped back in Pathoumsat's car and the youths sped off. Other motorists followed and noted the fleeing vehicle's license plate number.

Meanwhile, Dan turned to his horrified wife and son and said, "I've been shot." He stripped off his shirt, revealing a small hole in his abdomen, then collapsed on the street. Witnesses rushed him to a nearby hospital.

He died the following morning at 6:27 A.M.[6]

Exactly nine months and one day after the fatal shooting, Sothsay Pathoumsat was found guilty of murder in a three-day adult court trial. He admitted he was a member of the Red Cobra, a sometimes-violent gang composed of Southeast Asian-American youths. Other gang members were in the car with him at the time of the shooting, drunk and allegedly "egging him on."[7]

WHAT'S GOING ON HERE?

And where did both of these tragic incidents take place? The hard streets of New York? The inner city of Los Angeles? The South Side of Chicago? A ghetto in some godforsaken metropolis?

No. Both events occurred within a few miles of each other in

Portland, Oregon, a mid-sized community consistently rated among the most "livable" cities in the United States. Portland—nestled against the Cascade Mountain chain in the beautiful Pacific Northwest, just southwest of the breathtaking Columbia River Gorge—has a worrisome problem with youth violence.

"In Chicago or Los Angeles, the assault [at Lloyd Center] might not have attracted much notice," wrote reporters George Rede and Erin Hoover Schraw of the Portland *Oregonian*. "But the brutality and the random nature of the attack touched a nerve in Portland and its suburbs."[8]

Reports like this do more than "touch a nerve" in my own soul. They tear it up. My heart aches to know that this great nation of ours is caught in the midst of an epidemic of violence that threatens to destroy us all. How can we hear such reports and remain unmoved?

The reporters conducted several "street interviews" to get the pulse of the community about the incident. Typical of the responses was this one by nineteen-year-old Damon Turner, who didn't condone the violence but was not surprised by it: "People... tend to think of Portland as a safer place [than other cities] and they're starting to realize over the last several years that maybe it's not."[9]

No, it's not. And contrary to what many of us might want to believe, neither are most other American cities. Consider just a few startling statistics:

- In the first half of 1994, the highest rates of homicide per 100,000 people were not found in New York City or Los Angeles, but in New Orleans (48) and Richmond, Virginia (38). Little Rock, Arkansas, had the highest rates of both burglary (1,774) and aggravated assault (1,145), while Beaumont, Texas, had the highest rate of rape (93 per 100,000 people).[10]

- The highest rates of violent crime per one thousand people in the first half of 1994 were in Newark, New Jersey (19.3), St. Louis, Missouri (18.1), and Atlanta, Georgia (17.9). Violent crime includes incidents of homicide, forcible rape, aggravated assault, and robbery.[11]

- In 1993—for the first time—Americans were more likely to be killed by a stranger than by a family member or friend. "Every American now has a realistic chance [of being murdered because of] the random nature the crime has assumed," according to the FBI's Uniform Crime Report for 1993.[12]

- There were 24,526 murders in 1993, up 3.2 percent from 1992.[13]

- Through June of 1994, murder rates rose 7.5 percent in cities of 100,000 to 500,000, while they soared 14 percent in cities of 50,000 to 100,000.[14]

- The USA's crime level—14.1 million reported in 1993—is larger than the population of many countries.[15]

- Gang killings are up 371 percent since 1980.[16]

- Sixty-eight percent of victims of gang killings were white; 69 percent were eighteen or older.[17]

- Murder arrests among people under eighteen years of age increased 128.1 percent from 1983 to 1992, while rape was up 24.7 percent and aggravated assault was up 95.1 percent.[18]

- Nearly a million teenagers are victims of violent crime each year.[19]

- Two-thirds of inner-city children in one Alabama survey reported being victims of at least one violent act, and 43 percent said they had witnessed a murder. One told of her weariness at "going home and spending the entire evening on the floor" to protect herself against stray bullets.[20]

- School violence led President Clinton to sign an executive order on October 23, 1994, that requires districts to expel for at least one year any student who brings a gun to school.[21]

Many years ago when I was working with David Wilkerson to found Teen Challenge, a powerful ministry targeted toward drug addicts, I began to feel restless in my spirit about the way morals and society were changing. *What's happening to our children?* I asked myself. *Violence is becoming a way of life for many of them, and violence only gives birth to violence. What kind of future lies ahead for them?*

In the 1960s I began to speak about the drug epidemic that I saw looming on the horizon. Perhaps at that time I did not have the experience and wisdom that I do now. Yet I was seriously looking at our children. Why? Because I too was a kid who came from a world that was afflicted by evil adults. These people were my role models—the drug addicts, the pushers, and the gang members. To me they looked successful. I got caught up in that lifestyle.

When I was converted, I became like a child again. I began to flash back and review the danger zones that had led me to such a lifestyle. My conclusion is that we must save and protect the kids of this nation. They are our future. Unless we understand the significant role our kids have to play, we will never restore the strength of our country.

Still, I never imagined that it would get as bad as it has become. I never dreamed that our children would pose our biggest dilemma.

People in the inner-city ghettos live with the knowledge that life in America cannot get any worse. Everyone is looking at them; they are living in glass houses. And because their problems are more obvious and out in the open, they seem to be dismissed by society.

The middle- and upper-class suburbs were content to let those in the inner city destroy themselves. When I first started warning America about the inner-city powder keg, no one projected that the ghettos' problems were going to become everyone's problems, including the suburbs'. Yet we can't blame the inner city and the ghetto. For them the main question is simply survival.

These people have lost hope. They have gone from helplessness to hopelessness. They are victimized by poverty and lack of education. Children in the ghettos don't have to go to Lebanon or Vietnam to see a war; they just have to look outside their bedroom windows. It's dog-eat-dog and children are numbed to the sight of death because they have seen it so many times. Love has ended; hate has begun. Regardless, they are survivors.

Since I knew what it was like to grow up without a family and surrounded by violence and evil, I determined that my own children would be shielded from all that. As my children were growing up, we always located in small cities so that they would be protected.

While I traveled to the big cities of America and the world, Gloria and my four daughters stayed at home. There I knew they would be protected, they would receive a good education, they'd have neighbors who watched out for one another. When I was on trips, I could be assured that our neighbors were looking out for my kids.

Such a strategy would no longer work. The violence has spread beyond the big cities to the suburbs and even rural communities. There's no such thing as a "safe city" anymore. There's nowhere to hide.

All over America, in big cities and towns smaller than ten thousand people, the spirit of violence has spread like a flock of vultures circling over places that once enjoyed peace. The gangs intend to take their fear and intimidation everywhere possible and take whatever they can get. They'll walk into a quiet neighborhood—into *your* neighborhood, even your own bedroom—put a gun to your head and pull the trigger, without thinking twice. Horrifying inci-

---

Surrounded by Terrorists

Whether we admit it or not, we're surrounded by terrorists. We're being hunted by violence. Families move from Beirut, only to discover that what they're fleeing is already here. This is ironic. Centuries ago the Puritans fled England to find a better life here, and they found it. Today we find ourselves in a mess. But what are we going to do? Should we pack up our stuff and move to a desolate land and start again? But where would we go? There's no place left.

I say, it's time to bring back the Bible. It's time to bring back prayer. These are the only things that still have the power to help make a people moral by connecting them to the Almighty. We have to be more evangelistic with our own kids, teach them to discover whether they have the gift of being a missionary or an evangelist. Our kids are under attack, so let's come up with a different form of attack. Let's rush to the battlefront with the weapons of the Spirit.

dents are taking place all over this country... and it's only going to get worse.

Gone are the days when gangs and youth violence were limited to the decaying inner cities of America. Consider the following:

- Denver now has six thousand gang members in a city of 500,000 people; gang-related incidents shot up 30 percent in the first nine months of 1993.

- Salt Lake City now has 1,760 gang members in a city of 160,000 people; gangs were unknown just five years ago. In the first six months of 1993, there were 72 drive-by shootings—more than double the number in all of 1992.

- In Longmont, Colorado, a small town thirty miles north of Denver, police have increased patrols and established a hotline to report handguns at schools.

- In Magna, Utah, gang graffiti mars buildings in the town's historic downtown. Houses have been shot up and residents are worried.[22]

Don't you dare underestimate the network of the gangs! Gang-run activity is all over this country. The gangs are a multibillion-dollar enterprise and the name of the game is drugs. The gangs are out to infiltrate our junior high and senior high schools to sell their poison to our children. Sometimes the biggest mafioso moves to a small town so he can't be located—but he still controls the drug trafficking. Today's gangsters are copying and updating the ideas and methods of the old-timers.

No town or city is safe from their influence. My own city of Colorado Springs, Colorado, is home to sixty-eight Christian ministries (at last count). Yet recently when police showed photographs of weapons confiscated from teenagers at our biggest mall, you could see piles of Uzi submachine guns, nine-millimeter pistols, and wicked-looking guns with souped-up clips. (The latter was taken from a fifteen-year-old kid this past Christmas Eve. Can you imagine the scene if he would have decided to use his gun before it was confiscated?) Today, wherever you go, you find scenes just like this. The cops are outgunned by little kids!

HOW COMFY ARE WE?

Perhaps there was a time not too long ago when many of us in the suburbs could stretch out in our easy chairs and tut-tut about the terrible violence taking over the ghettos and barrios of America. We didn't have to worry much about gangs or youth violence because those awful things plagued the inner city, not us. The harsh reality is that senseless killings and unchecked violence rendered many of us incapable of loving and caring for these people. We might even have thought that "those people" deserved everything they got, and that if they didn't want to live like that anymore, why, they should just move.

We can't be so complacent anymore. Gangs and youth violence are here, among us. Whether we live in the city or in the suburbs, in a heavily populated urban area or on a farm in the country, in the Northeast or the Northwest or the South or the Rocky Mountain states, it's long past time for us to sit up and take notice.

Even the Mafia is scared. One mobster has been quoted as saying, "If we don't do something to deal with the gangs today, they're going to rise up and kill us all tomorrow."

My friends, I would never write this book just to scare you. But I have a job to do. The church of Jesus Christ must wake up from its deep slumber. There is a war going on, with real bullets that take real lives, and somehow we've been dreaming of sugarplums. It's time that we woke up.

There is so much that we can do! I remember when Gloria and I first returned to New York City after Bible school. We were attending a small Spanish church. Gloria was moved by the many kids who were in the projects in the neighborhood around the church. No one at the church was doing anything significant to reach out to these kids. Then, like now, most churches were content to settle for whoever enters the doors and made little effort to actually go out and "compel them" to come in. Gloria decided that something needed to be done.

So one summer day, she enlisted the help of about five or six teenage girls from the church to help her with an outreach into the projects. They went door to door inviting the kids to come out for a time of music and stories. They concentrated on an area one block wide. The first week they coaxed about twenty-four kids, between five and twelve years of age, to come and join in a song service. The kids were then treated to Bible stories.

A Few Safety Tips

The following safety tips may seem like common sense, but many people would not even think of them.

1. At night, you should always park near a light.
2. *Never* allow yourself to be coaxed into an argument or confrontation with young kids—so many of them have no regard for life. Gang initiations often involve the potential gang member finding an innocent victim at random. Some current gang initiations you should be aware of:

    A. A carload of gang kids, initiates, will drive at night with their headlights off. The first person who sees them coming and tries to flash their lights, as a courtesy, to let the car know that its lights are off, is the one gang members select as their victim. It is completely senseless and at random. Gang members will then follow the car and quite often murder the person(s).

    B. A young girl wanting to join a gang, or get "jumped in," is required to have sex, often in succession, with the male members of the gang.

    C. Potential gang members are sometimes required to prove their courage by having sex with someone who is known to have AIDS.

These are just a few examples of gang initiations. They vary all over the country.

The bottom line here is, BE CAREFUL. Realize that times have changed and that you have to act accordingly. Think ahead and you'll greatly reduce your chances of becoming a victim of gang violence.

The next week, forty-eight adventurous kids came out to hear Gloria and the teenage girls. By the third week, Gloria and her small team had nearly seventy kids to handle. These were unruly street kids, most of whom had never stepped foot inside a church building. The teenage girls were now doubling as crowd control specialists. At this point, Gloria turned over the program to the church, which assumed responsibility for its continuation.

My point is not to highlight what a great person Gloria was (and is), but to show that evangelism does not have to be complicated. Everyone can and should do it. All it takes is a concern and a burden for what you see going on around you... and then doing something about it.

The real question is, how many skeletons is our country going to keep in the closet, hoping that the problem will just go away? Let me tell you, it is never going to just go away. We need to realize this now. We cannot allow ourselves to be oppressed by such an apathetic spirit of denial. If we do, then we who know the Light of the world will begin to live by the standards of this age and give in to helplessness and acceptance of whatever comes our way.

We must say no! We have the answers.

Youth violence has reached epidemic proportions in this country. And so far, too much of the church has been asleep. My goal in this book is not only to wake us all up to the reality of what's going on, but to offer some real hope about what we can do. There is still time to save our youth... and ourselves.

If we fail to do anything, the future is nothing short of frightening.

CHAPTER 2

The Holy Ghost Hospital

The world is full of forgotten, hurting people. Many are in such pain that no anesthetic known to man can begin to reduce their agony. Hardened sinners, new Christians, nice people who don't know the Lord—they're all the targets of massive hurt, pain, and sorrow. And the great sadness is that they don't know where to turn.

Oh, they have turned to the professionals, to the greatest "experts" this country has to offer. They line up at the couches of the psychologists and psychiatrists who spend long years of study to find out how to heal the wounds of these desperate, hurting men and women.

And yet the pain only gets worse.

I can't help but ask: Where is the church of Jesus Christ? The church is one of the biggest organizations in the world; surely it has the resources to make a difference for good on this hurting planet? Surely it can provide some measure of healing?

No one doubts that God has given the church a tremendous place of ministry to help and to heal the wounded people of the world. God calls us to be his Holy Ghost Hospital. When the bullets fly and the blood spills, he expects us to rush the wounded to intensive care. When hearts are broken and all hope seems lost, he has privileged us to deliver Christ's soothing message of reconciliation, love, and peace with God.

Yet something has gone wrong.

CLOSED DOORS AND EMPTY EMERGENCY ROOMS

For many years, I have been forced to wake up to the painful truth that Christianity in the United States has largely turned away from its God-given mission. The doors to the hospital have been closed and the emergency room has filled with cobwebs. No longer would most of us give up everything just to live in the days of the Book of Acts, when the church "turned the world upside down" and exploded in size despite intense persecution from the devil. No longer are we like the believers in those early days, when the Holy Spirit completely possessed the life of the church and filled its members with love and power and an attractive, humble spirit. No longer do we seem willing to move wherever God directs, to reach out to people in the compassion of Jesus himself. Holiness and godliness marked everything those first believers did; now we just read about such things. Something entirely different seems to mark our own days.

Today we live in the age of entertainment. Never in the history of the church have we been more absorbed in entertaining ourselves. The world can go to hell, but we will insist on having a good time.

Evangelism has been replaced by things that are more luxurious and "feel-good" than sharing the gospel. We have been seduced by such things as prosperity, new doctrines, hyper-faith. We have been distracted by seminars and conferences. I believe that these things, balanced with everything else that the Bible teaches, are not bad in and of themselves. But they are symptomatic of a deeper problem. They signify a lack of commitment. It's easy to have Bible studies and prayer meetings. It does not take great faith and commitment to attend a seminar. But to set ourselves to reach the lost and save this nation takes great, consistent commitment and putting our lives and faith into action.

Sheer commitment alone can accomplish great things, even though they may not be good things. In 1917 Vladimir Lenin took over Russia with only forty thousand followers, and within a few decades communism controlled one-third of the earth's population. How did this happen? Through committed young followers, like the young man who wrote the following letter to his fiancée:

We have been described as fanatics. We *are* fanatic. Our lives are dominated by one great overwhelming factor—the struggle of world communism. It is my life, it is my people, my religion, my habit, my sweetheart, my wife, my mistress, my bread, and my meat. I work for it in the daytime, I dream of it at night. I cannot carry on a friendship, a love affair, or even a conversation without relating to the force that both guides and drives my life. I have already been jailed because of my convictions, and if necessary, I am ready to go before a firing squad.

We Christians supposedly number in the millions here in the United States alone. Yet with our large numbers, we are unable even to touch and control the problems in our own nation. The communists were willing to die for their cause, but we seem unwilling to die for Jesus. Death should mean nothing to us, only resurrection!

The church once had such commitment as this, but no longer. Why this change? What happened? Why do we love our television sets more than our neighbors?

I think part of it is because we want to feel safe. We are scared to death to bring into the light all these hurts and pains and frustrations and rejections that fill the lives of dejected men and women all around us. We don't want to deal with the nasty people who hurt us and who step on us. And if the truth be known, we don't want to acknowledge the people whom *we* hurt and whom *we* treat so badly. It's safer and more comfortable to stay inside our four walls and be entertained. If you turn up the volume loud enough, you don't have to listen to the weeping and the screams of agony piercing the air outside.

Men and women, the church was never meant to be an entertainment center. The church was created to be a Holy Ghost Hospital. We have been commissioned by Jesus himself to leave our comfortable easy chairs behind and instead go out into the hurting world and tend to the wounded. If we don't, who will? Who can?

This is one of the most urgent messages I have ever presented to the body of Christ. All around the world, violence and terror and pain have become a way of life for millions of men and women made in God's image. Gangs have transformed peaceful neighborhoods into war zones. Teenagers and even preteens are shooting each other in horrifying numbers. Mothers and fathers are even killing their own babies.

If ever this world and this nation needed the Holy Ghost Hospital, it's now.

Yet not only have we traded in our scalpels and our sutures for TV remote controls and bags of Cheetos®, but we have gone out of our way to shoot our own wounded!

Please Don't Shoot! I'm Already Wounded: The Story of a Heartbreak and a Ministry was the title of a beautiful book published several years ago, written by a well-known Christian lady who survived the horrors of Hitler's Germany. In the middle of that ugly, ruthless

---

Kids and Violence

Just after the Rodney King verdicts helped to spark the Los Angeles riots which destroyed large parts of South Central L.A., columnist Debra J. Saunders from the *Los Angeles Daily News* wrote, "Call Los Angeles Not Yet Beirut. A sprawling town where two wrongs do more than make a right, they beget 20 wrongs.... many corpses. Homes burned. Jobs gone. Peace of mind, up in smoke. What next?... The temptation is strong for each community to hunker down and burrow in familiarity. But that tendency only can lead to more division—African-American against Korean. Latino against African-American. White against minority. Such insularity can only make it easier for gangs to pick us all off, block by block.... If Los Angeles decides to go on trying to contain crime in poor neighborhoods, we are in for a reckoning. Crime is the enemy. And this city will either tackle it wholesale, or succumb to the flames."[S1]

I agree with Saunders that we have to take action. But who are we going to call? Can the Ghostbusters help us? Of course not. The real question is, are we going to allow these negative stories to move us to positive action? The church must begin to work in concert with the "gatekeepers" of our cities—with police, with school officials, with the politicians. We must tell them we want to work together to achieve a spiritual and social conscience. We must work hand in hand. The problem is an empty hole in the souls of our youth that only God can fill.

regime, Maria Anne Hirschmann came to experience the grace and the love of God and saw the Lord heal so many of her terrible memories.

After her book was published, this woman became recognized in many parts of the world as an outstanding Christian spokesperson. Then one day a personal tragedy struck and her husband walked out of her life. Without any discussion, without even saying a word, he walked away and left her alone. She found herself abandoned. But that was not the worst of it.

Wherever this lady tried frantically to explain to the Christian public what had happened to her, she was slapped with rejection. A wall of indifference rose around her—impenetrable, heartless, stifling. Here she was, a victim of abandonment, and yet Christians would not open their arms to receive her and heal her.

In the end, we stopped hearing from this lady altogether. Her wounds grew so deep that she gave up her writing career and retreated into her own little world. Right now she is living somewhere in a remote corner of Switzerland.

And still she bleeds.

Instead of giving life to the fallen, hurting soldiers of the cross, much of the time the church just finishes them off. I have heard it all too often: "When I was desperate for help, no one reached out to me. All those people in the church did was criticize. Why should I waste my time there?" One lady actually said to me, "I find more compassion at the local bar than in the church."

What a terrible indictment! What a horrible truth! We have all heard that the church is the only army that shoots its wounded. That is not a good reputation for us!

That's the reason why, with everything that's in me, I am pleading for the body of Christ to reopen the doors of the Holy Ghost Hospital. People are wounded and hurt and they need to check in. We *must* help them, we *have* to regain the sensitive spirit that will let people know they are going to be loved, cared for, forgiven, and warmly welcomed.

A MESSAGE FOR ALL OF US

This is a message for all of us in the body of Christ. It is not a message only for Baptists or Methodists or Presbyterians or Catholics or Lutherans or Pentecostals. The Holy Ghost Hospital needs all the doctors and nurses and orderlies it can find. Maybe your M.D. degree (Doctor of Mercy) is from the University of Arminianism. Great! We need you. Maybe you hold a Ph.D. degree (Doctor of Philanthropy) from the Calvinist School of Deep Theology. Wonderful! We need you too. Or maybe you don't have any degrees at all, but you can fill a bucket and push a mop. Fabulous! We can't do without you. The truth is, the church *as a whole* must become once more what it was meant to be: the Holy Ghost Hospital. Accept your calling and report for duty. We'll find a floor where you can serve!

One thing that has always touched me so deeply about our leader, Jesus Christ, is described in chapter seventeen of the Gospel of John. Four times our Master cried out in tremendous compassion to his heavenly Father. He came with a wonderful request. He asked "that all of them may be one, Father, just as you are in me and I am in you. May they also be in us so that the world may believe that you have sent me.... May they be brought to complete unity to let the world know that you sent me and have loved them even as you have loved me" (Jn 17:21-23). Four times he made the identical request. He told his men that the world would know they were his disciples by the love they expressed to one another.

My friends, do we recognize the awesome power of the unity of the body of Christ? Jesus was not talking here about denominations. He wasn't talking about Baptists, Presbyterians, Methodists, or Lutherans. He was not talking about Catholics or the Disciples of Christ. He wasn't talking about Pentecostals or charismatics. That was never his intention. Jesus prayed four times with all his heart— he repeated it so we could get it in our hearts and in our minds— that we should all be one. *One.*

What unimaginable power there is in unity! Oh, what the Holy Ghost Hospital could accomplish if all of us were working together!

Think of it: ministers of healing from all kinds of churches and all races and all social and economic backgrounds, taking Jesus' words seriously and moving out into the streets to tend to the bloody wounds of hurting people trapped in the devil's clutches. Holy Ghost Hospital ambulances rushing the critically injured into the arms of the Great Physician, Jesus Christ. Bold, fearless, filled with tender compassion for the spiritually dying, we move out as a great army of the Lord into the camp of the enemy.

When pastors and church leaders begin to teach and preach a message of unity and oneness in Christ, this country will see the power and the love that is in Jesus. This is the spiritual "love affair" that is missing. It is a love affair in which we begin to supply the lifeblood to the veins of those people who are working hard in the field of harvest abandoned by most of the church—the inner cities and the gangs.

This is the mighty army that we should be. Yet this mighty army is secluding itself in the mountains. But beware: The inner city will soon find its way to the mountaintop; it is already very close. It is already infiltrating the outskirts of suburbia. The inner city is dying, so where will it go? It will steal the food, the money, and the houses—everything—from the people on the mountaintop. The gangs in the valley will arise slowly but surely to conquer.

What is the reason we have so much division? You know the answer: flesh! One man within a movement begins to disagree with the leader of that movement, then he infiltrates the camp and begins to sweet-talk the people. He starts to push his own way, his own revelation, to the people. Some of them believe what he says, so eventually he brings division, takes a crowd, and creates another denomination: "This is my denomination; this is the way we believe. The rest of you just don't get it."

God never intended for us to go down that road. Never! He wants us to be *one*. He wants us to know that the only way we will be able to help this dying world is to understand his heartbeat, his compassion, his purpose. And that is that we are *one*.

Most churches want to grow, but they want new members who are already saved. They want people who have something to offer.

They don't want to have to deal with new converts off the street—that's too messy and too uncomfortable. The spirit of unity in Christ is what the world needs to see in us. With unity we can confuse everyone in the world who thinks that we don't work together or get along. We should put our differences aside and not let anyone change us or distract us from unity. We must let Jesus Christ be the common denominator, the bond that holds us together, regardless of our denomination.

The Holy Ghost Hospital was his idea, not mine!

Romans 15:1 describes God's heartbeat and compassion and purpose better than I could ever hope to. Paul writes, "We who are strong are to bear with the failings of the weak and not to please ourselves." Do you think you are strong? Then you are to bear with the failings of the weak. You say that doesn't please you? So what? If you are really strong, that won't matter. There are a lot of things that must be done in the Holy Ghost Hospital that may not please us. Bedpans have to be changed, vomit must be cleaned up. But so what? Our job is to help the weak become strong—not to abandon them because they are weak.

Then consider Galatians 6:1: "If someone is caught in a sin, you who are spiritual should restore him gently." This is a great passage for workers in the Holy Ghost Hospital! Gentleness means everything in hospital work. You don't rip off bandages to change the dressing; that only tears bigger wounds. You don't drop somebody on a gurney and heave them down the hall, hoping that they crash into the right room. The wounded need tender, gentle care. And that's what spiritual people are called to give.

WHO'S REALLY SPIRITUAL?

There's sometimes a problem with this word "spiritual." Some way, somehow, we have misunderstood what the word means. There are a lot of "spiritual" people out there who take this verse in Galatians out of context. They look down on people constantly. They look down on them so strongly that instead of building them up, they hurt them. I've never been able to figure this out, but they actually try to be more spiritual than Jesus Christ! They are so "heavenly minded," so "spiritual," that they have no spiritual sensitivity about the needs of others. Sometimes they float so high that they never touch the ground, where people live.

And the result? People die. These "spiritual" giants can't even see the hurting man or woman breathing right in front of their faces. They don't see them! And why not? Because they are so "spiritual." They feel so superior to the average person. That's why they never touch the real needs of the hurting people around them.

We know Jesus was called "the friend of sinners," but I doubt many observers would accuse the church of that today. Not only are we not the sinners' friends, we make it clear we don't like them very much. They're too dirty. Too crude. Too nasty. Too dangerous.

Do you know what the root of this problem is? It's a false idea of holiness. People who think like this completely misunderstand holiness. They think holiness means they are to be jealous only for right doctrine and practice. They think they are defending Jesus Christ. But what kind of doctrine did Jesus Christ have? "This is my command: Love each other" (Jn 15:17). False holiness results only in rudeness and arrogance.

I knew of a young girl, a talented musician, who wore makeup and kept her hair short. She was hired to play the piano at a church. A lady in that church didn't approve of either makeup or short hair on women, so she complained to the pastor. "You can't hire her," she asserted. "She has short hair and makeup!"

"I didn't hire her hair to play the piano, I hired her hands to play," responded the pastor. The lady left the church.

I was born again through a Pentecostal ministry. But my first experience in a Pentecostal church was horrible. I was just born again, a babe in Christ. And the very first Sunday I went to church I had an ugly confrontation with a believer.

Now, remember my background. I never was taught proper Christian manners. I didn't know how to conduct myself. I hardly had the manners to know how to eat, how to hold a fork. So one Sunday morning I came walking into this church with my long hair and moving like a jitterbug. Seventy-five or eighty of my guys came along with me. They, at least, wanted to respect me by attending a church with me. (It sure wasn't their own idea to go!) I'm sure it was the largest crowd that pastor ever had in his entire life!

I'll never forget my first impression of the church. One old lady, whom I viewed as representing all Christians, came up to me and accused, "What are you doing with that long hair? Go outside and cut your hair! This is the house of God!"

I couldn't believe it. "What?" I stammered.

"This is the house of God," she repeated. "Go get your hair cut!" There wasn't a whiff of compassion in her voice—just cold, hard, angry indignation.

You know, I never thought the church of the Lord was a barber shop. My problem wasn't in my hair, it was in my head.

I walked into church that day, only to be rudely confronted. "Walk this way! Don't do that! Don't you know where you are?" Is that the way we talk to a person? Hey, we don't need to be a Christian to act like a gentleman or a lady. We've got to get that in our heads.

How sad. I had just come into the church, and the first person to greet me made me feel as if I were nothing. Her rule of "holiness" said, "If you don't talk this way or behave this way, you are not a Christian." She never bothered to find out that I had just left a violent life in the gangs. It never occurred to her that I needed love and understanding. Instead, she pushed me away.

Friends, there is a better way to get to somebody. There's something about honey that brings the flies in!

THE MEEKNESS OF HOLINESS

We have a big problem with "rough" holiness without virtue. Somehow we have come to think of holiness only in terms of what we don't do: we don't wear our hair long, we don't wear certain kinds of clothes, we don't hang out in certain places, we don't have certain kinds of friends, we don't do this and we don't do that. And

A Living Nightmare

In early 1995 investigative journalist Bill Moyers took a four-hour, in-depth look at violence in America and what we can do about it. Moyers talked to convicted criminals and innocent victims, police officers and government officials, educators and experts to try to bring some understanding to a frightening but often baffling problem. It was a fascinating report.

The Sunday before his program aired on PBS, Moyers published an article in *Parade* magazine that previewed some highlights from the show. He ended his article by writing this:

> Two years ago, the National Research Council completed a massive study on violence, concluding: "Full understanding of the causes of violence will not be achieved in the foreseeable future—nor is that understanding necessary in order to make progress in reducing violence. A successful intervention at just one point in a long causal chain can prevent some events or reduce their consequences."

Moyers concluded his article by commenting, "I believe this is so. And I see no alternative but to act on it. Otherwise, our collective future truly will become a living nightmare."[51]

It doesn't take a genius to see that Bill Moyers is right. And "nightmare" is not too strong a word. After spending more and more of my time in the inner cities of America, both large and small, there is no question in my mind that Moyers is absolutely on target. He was addressing the nation, but my job is to speak specifically to the church of Jesus Christ. And I have a question to ask.

If we in the church do nothing to stem the rising tide of youth violence in this nation, to what can we look forward? If we continue to stay within the safe, four walls of our comfortable congregations and refuse to get involved, what kind of a society will we be helping to create? What kind of future are we handing to our children?

heaven help the brother or sister who does! There are only too many of the brethren who will be very happy to point out the errors of their "sinning" brothers and sisters!

We have forgotten about the meekness of holiness. Nobody would question that Moses was a very holy man—God said he talked with him face to face, like a man does with his friend—and yet the Bible says that "the man Moses was very meek, above all the men which were upon the face of the earth" (Nm 12:3, KJV). This very holy leader was not anxious to blast the wandering Israelite who, in the opinion of some, might have gotten out of line.

One time God's Spirit came in power upon seventy elders of the people and they began prophesying in Moses' presence. A few moments later a report came in that two men were prophesying in the middle of the camp, apart from Moses' group. Joshua was angry at this breach of church etiquette and said, "Moses, my lord, stop them!" But how did Moses respond? He replied to his young friend, "Are you jealous for my sake? I wish that all the LORD'S people were prophets and that the LORD would put his Spirit on them!" (Nm 11:28, 29).

Holiness wrapped in meekness is a powerful package, not a weak one. That is why Paul wrote, "The Lord's servant must not quarrel; instead, he must be kind to everyone, able to teach, not resentful. Those who oppose him he must gently instruct, in the hope that God will grant them repentance leading them to a knowledge of the truth, and that they will come to their senses and escape from the trap of the devil, who has taken them captive to do his will" (2 Tm 2:24-26).

Holiness will stand for what's right and will not budge or compromise; but it does so gently. It may receive blows for taking such a stance, but it will never give them. The kind of holiness that we so desperately need today in our churches and in the country at large is the kind that comes from the fear of God. A holy person fears God; an unholy person does not. It is the lack of this holy fear of God that is destroying America.

If we are to reopen the Holy Ghost Hospital, if we are to reach out beyond ourselves to tend to the hurting and the dying, we can't afford this kind of total rudeness, this roughness of "holiness." We can't expect those who have known nothing but the gangs to act like mature Christians. For a while, they will act like the people they have been. I did! But that's no reason to reject them or to stay in our comfortable homes and churches, imagining that they only get what they deserve.

HOLINESS, JESUS STYLE

One time Jesus and his disciples were on their way to Jerusalem but had to pass through Samaritan territory. Jesus sent a few of his men ahead into a town to prepare for his arrival that evening, but when the townspeople learned he was going to Jerusalem, they refused to welcome him. James and John, who were called "the sons of thunder," took it as a great insult and asked Jesus, "Lord, do you want us to call fire down from heaven to destroy them?" Oh, how they were hoping for a simple "yes"! So of course Jesus replied, "Sure, go ahead; the wicked wretches deserve all the misery they can get."

Is that what he said? No way! He sternly rebuked his own men and said, "You do not know what kind of spirit you are of, for the Son of Man did not come to destroy men's lives, but to save them" (Lk 9:51-55).

The disciples forgot for a moment that they were workers in the Holy Ghost Hospital and instead imagined that they were drafted into the Heavenly Bomber Corps! Or maybe they just forgot who the real enemy was. They thought the Samaritans were the enemy; Jesus knew they were the victims. Satan was the enemy, not people in need of Christ.

Do we make the same mistake?

We too forget that people are hurting. Because we are so "spiritual," we want people to act just like us. But none of us can ever take the place of Jesus Christ; the heart of Jesus is that people will be like him. And how did the Master act? He had compassion for lost people, who were "like sheep without a shepherd." He loved them. He cared for them. He spent himself for them. And ultimately, he died for them.

Jesus is our chief example of the gentleness of holiness at work!

Ephesians 4:32 says it like this: "Be kind and compassionate to one another, forgiving each other, just as in Christ God forgave you." What did kindness mean for Christ? Did he reach out to us after we had cleaned ourselves up and gotten ourselves all nice and presentable? Or did he leave the glories of heaven to take on human flesh and become one of us, to live where we live, to feel what we feel, and then give his life for us that we might have his life in us? Notice what this verse tells us to do: Just as God was kind to us and forgave us in Christ, so are we to be kind to others and forgive them.

No Fear of Death

Violence strips youngsters of their innocence, of their hope, and ultimately of their very souls. Unchecked, the rising tide of youth violence, gangsterism, and mind-numbing drugs will destroy the young people of this country... and everything else along with them.

Recently, a New York publishing house acquired worldwide rights to *Monster: The Autobiography of an L.A. Gangmember*. The book, written completely by hand in prison, tells the frightening story of Kody Scott, a member of the Eight-Tray Gangster Crips who shot his first victim at the age of eleven. In his book, Kody (also known as Sanyika Shakur) says that his grim early years turned him into a person who "didn't care one way or another about living or dying" and who "cared less than that about killing someone."[S1]

"Monster's" words reaffirm for me that many of our kids are not afraid of death—they're afraid of life. Meaning and purpose and value and beauty have been sucked out of their lives and they feel as though they're drifting aimlessly across a vast, stinking cesspool. Why should they care about killing someone else? They're not terribly concerned if they should die themselves.

But we cannot be kind to others without going to them. We cannot mail kindness to them in a shoe box. We have to go.

Paul said the same thing in 2 Corinthians 10:8. He told the Corinthians—a difficult bunch of people, by the way—that the Lord had given him great authority "for building you up rather than pulling you down." There are at least three ways to build somebody up:

1. Strengthen them.

2. Encourage them.

3. Comfort them.

Paul tells us that his authority was given to him by God to build up others. That's the reason we need a hospital so badly. We need a hospital because people are hurting and dying in front of our very eyes. Christian people, your brothers and your sisters, are wounded and hurt. Non-Christians, people who don't yet know the Lord— some of whom are even now in the gangs and in all kinds of desperate poverty in the inner city—are also wounded and hurt. All of them need a place where they can get treatment, where they can know they are loved and cherished and valued.

You know what America needs most today? It doesn't need more television stations or radio stations or shopping malls or multiplex theaters. What it needs is a Holy Ghost Hospital, run by caring and obedient members of the church of Jesus Christ. The needs have never been greater than they are today. We must get back to basics because the patient load already is staggering and growing every day.

We can't afford to shoot our own wounded anymore. We don't have the luxury of spending our resources sniping at other believers who differ with us on some point of doctrine or practice. We're in a war, and we've got to realize who the real enemy is.

DON'T WASTE YOUR AMMUNITION

In the early 18th century, the British army sent a troop ship to conquer Quebec, Canada, a prized French colony. An officer named

Captain Montgomery was in command of the expedition. When the British arrived, they anchored their ship in a spot where they could see a large Catholic church off in the hills. Outside the church stood a forest of statues depicting Catholic saints.

The enlisted Brits began to drink and soon got carried away. They approached Captain Montgomery and asked him if they could leave the ship to shoot up the statues—you know, to send a message to the Catholic church. In a moment of vulnerability, Captain Montgomery gave his permission. So his men left the ship and started shooting left and right. They blew away the body and head of St. Anthony; over there they pulverized St. Paul; next to him they blew St. Peter to bits. They were having a good time blasting away and were mightily rejoicing in their destructive efforts. Everybody was so happy to show the French who was boss.

But suddenly the French made an appearance. And by that time, the British had run out of ammunition.

I wonder how often we do that? We waste all our energy and all our bullets, throwing away all the power that God has given us to build up each other so that we come to unity. And then we wonder why the devil has such an easy time of mopping us up.

Listen, we have a real enemy to fight; don't fight with your sister or your brother! If you have any ammunition and any energy to fight, you'd better fight the devil.

Right now we're facing one of the greatest crises in the history of the church. Our youth are at grave risk. Violence is spiraling out of control in our cities and is spilling over into our suburbs and rural communities. New and ever more powerful drugs are sweeping the country and are taking the precious lives of our children. Our emergency rooms are busy round the clock with the victims of shootings, knifings, and beatings.

In a crazy world like that, the doors of the Holy Ghost Hospital *have* to be open, and every floor *has* to be fully staffed.

We don't need to fight our sisters and our brothers. We'd better be fighting the number-one enemy, the devil and his demonic cohorts. That's who we have to fight!

TRUE LOVE GIVES

I was very touched by a story I read in the newspaper a few years ago. It taught me a lesson about compassion that I can never forget. A fourteen-year-old girl by the name of Donna was afflicted with a serious medical condition. Without a heart transplant, she would not survive. Her fifteen-year-old boyfriend, Felipe, loved this girl deeply. He made it known that if anything were ever to happen to him, he wanted his heart to be given to his girlfriend.

One day Felipe was involved in a terrible accident in which a blood vessel in his head ruptured. Within a week, he died. True to his wishes, doctors took his heart and transplanted it into his girlfriend, giving her new life.

You know, the church of Jesus Christ is to be like that boy. The church of the Lord is a living force, not an institution or a building. It is you as an individual. You were given new life so that you could give that life to others. You were given a new heart so that your heart could be transplanted into somebody else.

Christian brother or sister, it is not for you to choke the life out of others. Jesus tells you to go—people are dying. Go to that gurney in the emergency room. You have the life in you so that you can give it to another. Lay your body right there on that gurney, extend your arms and tell that doctor, "Here, I want to give life to that person. Here is my blood; give my blood to that person." Extend your arms! You have the power to give spiritual blood that will allow others to live.

Jesus Christ himself told us, "You are weak, I am strong. I'm a spiritual man—here, take my life. It's all right!"

If we are truly spiritual, we know that we're plugged into the veins of Jesus Christ and we can therefore follow his example. I know that I'm plugged into the heartbeat of my compassionate Master. And because he's alive, he has caused me to be resurrected in him so that no matter how weak my body might be, I can help others find real life. So can you.

But you have to extend your arms. You have to be willing to put yourself on that gurney. You must entrust yourself to the

Resurrected One who promises to raise us up at the last day.

You know, it's not really a sacrifice to give yourself in service to the Master. We're not really giving up anything when we choose to obey him and leave behind our comforts and our safety to do our jobs in the Holy Ghost Hospital. Why not? Because in him, we have been given everything:

> Whatever was to my profit I now consider loss for the sake of Christ. What is more, I consider everything a loss compared to the surpassing greatness of knowing Christ Jesus my Lord, for whose sake I have lost all things. I consider them rubbish, that I may gain Christ and be found in him.   **Philippians 3:7-9a**

> In Christ all the fullness of the Deity lives in bodily form, and you have been given fullness in Christ, who is the head over every power and authority.   **Colossians 2:9-10**

Jesus Christ was the biggest hospital that ever existed on this earth. He was a walking hospital! He healed frantic people who for years had searched in vain for a cure. He brought hope to the hopeless, peace to the tormented, and sanity to the insane. Everything he did with his life proved all the claims he made for himself. Do you know what he did best? It was so beautiful. He spent his life checking people into their heavenly mansions.

JESUS, THE HOLY GHOST HOSPITAL

On the mean streets of life lived a lady who was caught up in open sin. The law required that she should be stoned until she was dead. The Pharisees caught her in bed with a man who was not her husband and so brought her to Jesus, asking him what they should do about it. They threw her in front of him, smugly waiting to see what he might say. Her situation was bad; Jesus was her only refuge. She had no way of knowing what Jesus would do.

Do you know what our Lord did for this woman? He laid his

reputation on the line. He heard the charge against her and started drawing something in the dirt. The crowd stood there in awe. Jesus didn't have to say a word. There was something about his character that paralyzed and froze the people. Nobody said anything; they just watched him write and write. What did he write? We don't know. But I think he began to write to those Pharisees and to their political system. He gave them a message in his own hand. He wrote everything that was going on at that time. He was telling the people, "Go ahead, check it out. Do you recognize that sin? How about that one? If you haven't done any of these things, then go ahead, you're spiritual—cast the first stone. Kill her! Go ahead."

But no one threw a single rock. One by one, they all dropped their stones and slithered away.

Finally, Jesus put his reputation on the line once more and said, "Woman, where are your accusers?"

"They're not here, Lord."

"Then go home and don't sin anymore."

Let's be honest: None of us is so different from that woman. Every one of us who is born into this world is infected with the disease of sin. All of us constantly have to go to the grace of God to ask for forgiveness. Through God's amazing grace we can ask that the blood of Jesus Christ would wash away our sins so that we can have fellowship with God once more. That is a promise for every believer, so we can have total, clean, uninterrupted communication with the Lord Jesus Christ.

Boys and girls in the gangs need this message of Good News. Where are they going to get it, if not from us?

People are hurting and dying without ever hearing of the love of God. Where are they going to hear about it, if not from us?

Men and women in your own city right now are in desperate need of a new heart, a heart not of stone but of flesh, a heart plugged into the veins of Jesus. Where are they going to receive one, if not in the Holy Ghost Hospital? If that hospital's doors are locked and bolted and chained, what are they going to do?

Or a better question: What are *you* going to do? I know what Jesus would do, because he did it all the time.

There was another incident with another lady. This lady was completely torn apart and hurt beyond words. She was a Samaritan, a girl we know as "the woman at the well." She was so ashamed. She had been sleeping with many different men. At one time she was married, but not anymore. Even so, she never went to bed alone. Naturally, she had a terrible reputation in town, and she knew it. Nobody had to tell her that she was living in sin.

One day, the walking hospital started looking for her. This lady was at her lowest point. She was so alienated, so hurt, so bruised, that she was completely lost. She was so ashamed of herself because she was the talk of the town. The old ladies used to come and gossip about her; they all thought they were so holy. They didn't know or care that she was hurting so terribly.

And then in walked a young man, about thirty-two years old. Right away he confused her when he asked for some water. No self-respecting man would do that with a sinful woman! That blew her away. But not only that—she knew Jesus was a Jew, while she was a gentile, a Samaritan. The two peoples weren't supposed to have anything to do with each other.

She was so mixed up; she could not conceive of somebody like Jesus. She had tried to sneak out to the well when everybody else was home eating, but there was Jesus, asking for water. She was amazed—and Jesus gave her just what she needed. He told her, "If you drink from the water I will give you, you will never be thirsty again." Then he described her whole sordid life to her. She was astonished and right there received a revelation. Her eyes were opened wide and she began to know that the one talking with her was God, Jesus Christ himself. The first thing this lady did was to run all around town, telling everybody about this new prophet who had given her new life.

What a hospital! What holiness! That's Jesus Christ.

A PLACE TO CHECK IN

I would never be where I am without that hospital. I have checked in many times since I became a Christian. I can think of five times in particular when I absolutely *had* to check in. Twice I was guilty and I knew it. I was bleeding, I was wounded, I had no energy. I was dying inside. My sins were like a dark cloud that cast long and menacing shadows over my soul. I had to check into the Holy Ghost Hospital. And I was healed.

The three other times, I was also wounded, hurt, bleeding—but this time at the hands of a fellow believer, one of my real heroes. He had given me life, and he had choked the life out of me. And when I needed him most, he wasn't there. Why not? Because he was so spiritual, so judgmental, so holy macaroni, that he didn't see I was dying. I needed him to lay his body right down beside me and give me a transfusion. I was gasping for air, I felt my whole life going to pieces... but he wasn't there.

It is bad enough when you are guilty, but when you are innocent and you are in agony and you are almost at the point of death—and yet nobody is there to check you into the hospital, its doors have been shut tight and locked—it's just too much.

Fortunately, I have other friends who also work at the Holy Ghost Hospital. They unlocked the doors and let me in. I checked into that hospital not too long ago, and I bawled my eyes out until I felt a great release. My brother embraced me, cried with me, hurt with me—and I was able to get on a plane a free man once more, healed, at peace, feeling great. That is what the Holy Ghost Hospital is meant to do.

My dear friends, this message is from my heart. It's not the message of an evangelist or a speaker or even an author. It's a heartfelt message from a Christian brother straight to you.

We are the body of Christ. We are blood-bought men and women who have been set free from the bondage of sin through the death and resurrection of God's only Son. The world needs us to take our places as faithful workers in the Holy Ghost Hospital. Our youth are dying. Our cities are dying. Our nation is dying. Spiritually speaking, it's Code Blue time and there's no time to waste.

It's either the Holy Ghost Hospital or the morgue. I know which one I have chosen. Will you join me?

CHAPTER 3

Where Have All the Families Gone?

In many ways, Houston, Texas, is a city under siege. Gang violence has spiraled out of control and city officials are scrambling to figure out how to solve the problem—or at least, how to keep it from growing.

A 1994 Houston Independent School District survey found that 70 percent of the district's students didn't feel safe at school. It's not hard to see why. Between September 1993 and May 1994 in the Houston schools, there were seventy-eight assaults with a weapon, 193 weapons violations, 447 incidents of disorderly conduct resulting in injury, and 671 nonweapon assaults.[1] "We have gone from fearing the Klan to fearing our own children," said Ernest McMillan, director of the Fifth Ward Enrichment Program, an anti-gang program in the heart of the city.[2]

Houston's church leaders recognized the urgency of their problem and, partly with that in mind, invited me to conduct a crusade in their city in the fall of 1994. I jumped at the chance. I love the sound of bullets—it lets me know that the devil is alive and that I'm going to go after him.

While I was in Houston for the crusade, the *Houston Chronicle* published a special fourteen-page report called "Seeds of Trouble." Its front page featured a photo of a teenager's shackled hands, jutting out from behind a prison door. Beneath the picture, set in "prison type," the report said, "Houston's teenagers are robbing, assaulting, and killing in ever-increasing numbers. Before we build bigger prisons to hold them, we should take a hard look at their lives and the problems that put them on a path toward crime. In the words of one researcher, violence does not drop out of the sky at age fifteen."[3]

The excellent special report told the wrenching stories of teen after teen who has felt tugged in the direction of the gangs. Teens with faces and names. Teens with all kinds of potential that may never be realized. Teens like these:

- Sweet-faced Bobby, experienced hijacker and long sexually abused by members of his stepfather's family. He now lives with his sister in a Spring Branch apartment, "the home they have made for themselves because their mother could not."[4]

- Eric, "who lives in a home that begs to be condemned, whose mother spent much of her time in beer joints."[5]

- Juan, "who was periodically kicked out of his home as a boy and left to sleep on the banks of the bayou."[6]

- Jamie, "who grew up among boys who learned early to take what they wanted."[7]

Sadly, these boys' stories are just a repeat of what's been happening for decades—only the names have changed. My mind races back to Hector, a member of the Mau Maus who was rejected by his parents but taken in by his uncle. Yet one day Hector took his uncle, tied him up, and beat him. We didn't allow that in the gangs—he didn't even give his uncle a chance to defend himself—and so we confronted Hector about it. "Well, he deserved it because he's an enemy, a member of my family," Hector said.

I remember a twelve-year-old who idolized gang members. Sometimes when we needed a quick escape we would jump from building to building over the top of the New York skyline. One day I noticed this kid following us, jumping between buildings. We were coming to a dangerous, long jump, and I turned around and ordered the kid not to follow... but he tried anyway. His little legs didn't allow him to make the leap and he missed the building, hurtling several stories to his death.

And I also think of my best friend Manny, whose addict father died of a heroin overdose and whose mother committed suicide a couple of months later. I could never understand why Manny continued to adore his father; I'd tell him to shut up when he started talking about how he missed both of them. At the time I thought it was a weakness. Now I know just how important a loving, intact family is.

All of these boys were and are examples of children hunting for love. The worst thing a kid can feel is lovelessness and hopelessness. Yet that's exactly what far too many of our kids are feeling every day.

The *Houston Chronicle* report attempted to explain many of the main causes of the city's teen violence problem. At least one of the reasons cited—perhaps the most significant of all—should come as no great surprise. It said the breakup of the traditional family provides a fertile recruiting ground for gang activity and youth violence.

"These children are not accidents of breeding," the report reminded its readers. "They are, by and large, the offspring of our most vulnerable population: people who are poor, uneducated, isolated, depressed, unemployed or marginally employed, and deeply pessimistic. They come, almost to a child, from families that are small disasters. Many have never known self-control or meaningful discipline. For students of the inner city, where much of America's youthful violence exacts its toll, the problem often comes down to ties that no longer bind. Children may feel only tenuously connected to their families and not so at all to any greater community, save perhaps a gang."[8]

It's easy to see why gangs can look like the easy way out of ghetto misery. Kids see fifteen-year-olds driving Porsches and wearing gold jewelry and expensive watches, and they identify with them—they're living the dream of the average ghetto dweller. Our kids look at a guy loaded with beepers and see that he doesn't need to work, yet he's making up to a thousand dollars a day, more money than the average middle-class executive. Many of the pimps I've met don't even know how to sign their names, yet they have the biggest bank accounts in the neighborhood. Kids look at these people and think, *I don't have any family; my new family is the gang, and it can give me all of this and more.* Suddenly they have a sister and a brother in the gangs that they never had before. And they soon take on the characteristics of their new "family."

The Arizona Criminal Justice Commission says, "Gang members, wannabes, and those students with a gang member in their family use alcohol and illicit drugs at rates far greater than the general population. The gang members and wannabes exhibit an almost cavalier, flippant attitude toward substance abuse, authority, and criminal activities. The similarities between self-proclaimed gang members and the students who say their family contains a gang member indicates the pervasive influence that family has on shaping attitudes and behavior. While there is some overlap between these two groups (that is, gang members with relatives in gangs), there are substantial numbers of youth who are not in a gang but who have a gang relative. These youth are at risk for developing a gang lifestyle. These results indicate that a critical period to reach youth is before they reach their preteen years, both in educating them to the hazards of gang life as well as the dangers of substance abuse."[9]

Sadly, this isn't only a Houston problem; it's the national norm. Since 1970, female-headed households with children under age eighteen have increased by 40 percent. Births to unwed teen mothers—the group most likely to wind up on welfare—tripled from 1961 to 1991. Those youngsters are precisely the ones who are least equipped to raise their own families. Consider that only 19 percent of youths referred to juvenile authorities for serious offenses in 1993 came from a home with both parents.[10] And did you know that over 70 percent of juveniles in state reform institutions come from homes without both parents present?[11]

I can't overstate how important the family is in combating the growth of gangs and teen violence. Families really are at the center of this problem. But don't take my word for it. Listen to the opinions of several police officers from around the country who specialize in gang intervention. We phoned several cities at random, so don't think this is a setup!

- Doug Allen, detective on the gang task force, Toledo, Ohio:
  "Kids often join the gangs because they are seeking attention and direction, things they aren't getting at home. Most of the gang members are from broken families who live in drug- and violence-infested areas. These families are usually socially dependent. Yet contrary to what might be expected, many of the kids who join the gangs are bright kids with plenty of potential to be productive citizens."

- Gary Ho, an officer in the gang enforcement section of the police department, Oakland, California:
  "My opinion is that the fault lies in the breakdown of the family and the inability of schools to assimilate these kids."

- Gary Leuthauser, day shift coordinator, gang enforcement unit, Denver, Colorado:
  "The family background of most gang members is as predictable as the day is long—bad family atmospheres with parents who may not be aware of what their kids are doing. The emphasis on gang prevention needs to be placed on young children. I am not optimistic at all that those who have entrenched themselves in the gang culture could or would ever get out. The only way we're going to have an impact on the gangs is to cut off the supply of members, which is the young kids."

- Pat Sardina, police force intelligence unit, Buffalo, New York:
  "Despite the usual profile of a gang member, some of these kids are well-educated and from decent families. Others, though, are from second- and third-generation welfare families and are in it for the money, because it allows them to do things and have things they could only dream of before."

- Buz Williams, gang enforcement unit sergeant, Long Beach, California:
  "The age group of sixteen to twenty-one is the most common in the gang culture, but there are some as young as nine and some older than twenty-one. I feel that the most effective way of deal-

ing with the gang problem is to reach the younger potential members before they become entrenched in the gang culture."

- **Todd Myers, police department gang unit, Austin, Texas:**
"Family-wise, there are some gang members who come from what we could consider 'decent' families, but most of them are from very negative family situations."

- **Jim Klisch, police department detective with the gang crimes/intelligence unit, Milwaukee, Wisconsin:**
"There is a serious problem with gangs in this city, and it's getting worse. It's expanding from being an inner-city problem and is now catching on statewide in smaller, white-bread communities. The problem has been driven by the deterioration of families, a loss of values, the growth of materialism, and lack of acceptance and identity. A great number of the gang members are from dysfunctional families, but some are just black sheep from what we might think of as 'good' families. There needs to be an improvement in social structure in order to combat the gang problem. That includes family structures and parenting skills with less emphasis on materialism. You've got the streets raising the kids; this is what we get when that happens."

- **Dave Starbuck, police department sergeant, Kansas City, Missouri:**
"A few years ago, the common denominator among almost all gang members was a dysfunctional, economically deprived family that was socially dependent. Now, more and more of the kids we encounter are from middle-class or upper-class families that appear to be solid family units. Their kids rebel and are fascinated with the dark side of society, something that is more and more common in our culture. The common thread now is anti-social attitudes and a lack of remorse or conscience. These kids have no problem with hurting or even killing innocent people."

Notice that even when the gang-related kids come from "good" homes, they're growing up without moral values. How good a home is that? Just because your belly is full and you have decent clothes doesn't mean your family is "good"; it may simply mean that you have enough money to be bad in more creative ways.

The biggest market for drugs today is not in the ghetto, but among the white middle class. Just as crack was designed for the ghetto, there are many drugs today that have been designed for the white middle class—PCP, crystal, LSD, and the new "designer" drugs. This is not a ghetto problem, but a people problem, a family problem, an educational problem. We need to rally together as a nation and get back to fundamental values that will enable us once again to become the "dream" nation of the world. Without deep cooperation between both spiritual and social agencies, working together as brother and sister, we can't hope to turn back the alarming statistics. But the most critical factor in turning back youth violence is found in the homes of America.

I could hardly believe the news item I saw a while ago datelined Sun Prairie, Wisconsin, a predominantly white suburb near Madison, the state capital. The headline read, "Mom urges son to attack neighbor kid."

Donna M. Streeter was charged with "second-degree recklessly endangering safety while armed" for encouraging her ten-year-old son to attack a neighbor boy with a pair of scissors. Sadly, it wasn't the first time she had encouraged her son's violence. On the previous day a neighbor says she saw this mother instruct her son to attack a nine-year-old boy. "What did he say to you?" Streeter asked her son about the other boy. "He asked me what my problem was," her son replied. "Well, you go punch him. Hit him in the face," she is alleged to have said—which the boy promptly did. He crossed the street to a bus stop and punched the other boy while his mother cheered, "That's it. Punch him good." Then Streeter herself crossed the street and yelled at the crying little boy. The next day, she gave her son a large pair of scissors and told him, "Now you go over there and get him." Fortunately, the nine-year-old was able to run away the second time and was uninjured.[12]

Reports like this confirm for me that this is a nation without heroes. We see here the essence of the problem. No longer are parents heroes; today they're accomplices, part of the problem. Of course, America still has a lot of good, decent parents. One of the trademarks of this country is that we are a decent and kind people. But today we are being overpowered by evil and we desperately need heroes.

We need heroic single parents who struggle to teach their kids morals and to go to church. Many of these people get by with two jobs. Their hearts are crushed under all their difficult circumstances. We need to step up and give these heroes a hand.

What do we expect from a kid who grows up without heroes? What kind of fathers will these boys be? They don't know how to be kind; they've never seen masculine kindness modeled for them.

We are the parents; we must be the heroes. The impressions we leave with our kids stay with them forever. Recently I took a short trip with my granddaughter. We had a great time together, talking, laughing, observing. On a deserted side street I pretended to let her drive while she sat in my lap. She clamped her little hands around the wheel while I continued to steer with a couple of fingers on the bottom of the wheel. She was having a ball—she really thought she was driving. It was the kind of tender moment that will be remembered forever. It was the kind of moment in which heroes are born.

I'll tell you frankly, I want to be the hero of my kids. I represent the masculine image to them, not some rock star or sports figure. When my daughter Nicole was young, I invented a story about the wolfman who got converted to Jesus. Even today, Nicole sometimes calls and wants to hear it to help her get to sleep. A number of years ago I came home from a long trip to Paris and became very upset when I found a large poster of Michael Jackson hanging up in her room. I tore down the poster and reminded her that Michael Jackson was not going to be her hero; I was. The next day I came home with a big poster of myself taken in Amsterdam, complete with big smile. I put that up in her room instead, and she didn't complain.

I tell that story to encourage you that we can be heroes if we try. I received a letter from a girl in Finland a little while ago, thanking me for talking about fathers as heroes. She said it changed the way she looked at her father. I get letters all the time from kids in juvenile detention and lockup who ask me in one way or another, "Can you be my dad?" That breaks my heart, because it shows me that these kids really want to do right, but they're prisoners of their own upbringing. They need a father, a dad who is a hero to them. We must be heroes to our kids! If we fail at this critical task, it is no wonder we are raising a generation of willing killers. The *Houston Chronicle* article quoted at the beginning of this chapter is right: These fifteen-year-old killers didn't just drop out of the sky.

Kids are starving for love, and they're not finding it at home. When our families fail at this most basic level, our kids begin to look for that love and acceptance with pseudofamilies—the gangs. Our children are vulnerable, and the gangs know it. I know it too because that's what happened to me.

"If I Grow Up..."

Alex Kotlowitz is a reporter for *The Wall Street Journal*. In 1991 he published a prize-winning book titled *There Are No Children Here*, a deeply moving account of the lives of two young boys growing up in desperate poverty on the South Side of Chicago. He took the title from a conversation he had with the boys' mother, LaJoe. When Kotlowitz told her he wanted to write a book about children in the projects, she replied, "But you know, there are no children here. They've seen too much to be children."[S1]

From an early age, LaJoe's boys—Lafeyette Rivers, then fifteen, and his brother, Pharoah, thirteen—were taught how to avoid neighborhood violence. It "is an integral part of their daily life, as routine as a trip to the mall in the suburbs. They know the rules of survival: at home, drop to the floor at the sound of gunfire; outside, look to see where the shots are coming from before running for shelter."[S2]

When they first met in the summer of 1985, Lafeyette even told Kotlowitz, "If I grow up, I'd like to be a bus driver." Unlike most children, he wouldn't think of beginning a sentence about his future with "when."[S3]

THE SON OF THE DEVIL

Nobody needs to tell me how important healthy families are to the emotional, physical, and spiritual well-being of children. People who have heard only a little of my story from bits and pieces of *The Cross and the Switchblade* or *Run, Baby, Run* probably know that I was one of the feared leaders of a violent New York gang, the Mau Maus. They probably know about my many scrapes with the law, about the fights, about the killings, and about the amazing efforts of a skinny white preacher from Pennsylvania, David Wilkerson, that finally resulted in my conversion to Jesus Christ. But they may not know about my nightmarish childhood in Puerto Rico that was largely responsible for shaping my violent teen years.

A few years ago my daughter Nicole sat down with me to ask some in-depth questions about my background. She has always had a fascination with her roots and she wanted to quiz me about my father and mother. I don't often open up about this period of my life; it's too painful. Some who hear me speak may assume that I am an extrovert, but I'm really not. Talking about those early years is difficult.

Nicole and I were alone and she began to dig in with her questions. As I began to go back in my mind to the years of my childhood, I had such a painful reaction to some of the memories that Nicole got scared. She began crying hard, because for the first time she became fully aware of the reality of my devastating background.

I was the eighth son born to Galo Cruz, a demonic spiritualist called an *espiritista*, and Aleja, his feared wife, a witch. My father was known throughout the area as "the Great One," a rural healer who communed with powerful spirits. We lived in a compound at Las Piedras, a peasant village in the shadow of El Yunque mountain in the Caribbean National Forest.

My father had great plans for me even before I was born—I was to take his place one day. But when I was two months old I became violently ill. I was quickly consumed to the bones and could not hold anything down in my stomach. No matter what spells my father cast, nothing worked. My father was going crazy with grief, but my mother was filled with anger. "He came to curse us!" she screamed at Papa. "He is the son of Satan!"

My father refused to listen to her, however, and despite her opposition, performed one of his most powerful and ancient rituals on my behalf. *And I got well!* Don't tell me the spirits are make-believe.

My father used to bathe me in all kinds of herbs in the belief that such "white" magic would protect me and make me strong. I believe that the devil was unable to kill me, not because of my father's efforts, but because I was born to serve the Lord. God would use the hardships and difficulties of my life to make me into a sensitive person who would fulfill his destiny by helping others in the power and name of Jesus.

From that day on, however, my mother began to hate me. I was severely abused—physically, emotionally, and verbally. *I* was the one who got whipped and threatened when she was angry with all the other kids (and eventually, there were seventeen others). *I* took the blame for everything.

Unsurprisingly, I became resentful and angry… and mean. I was in constant trouble at school, and the teachers grew afraid of me. Then when I was eight years old, an especially ugly confrontation with my mother changed my life forever.

One day, from what seemed to be out of nowhere, she screamed at me, "I hate you! I don't love you. You have been cursed from the day you were born! I hate you! You aren't my son. You are the son of Satan! Get out of this house! I don't want to see you!"

Her hateful words consumed my very soul. In a moment, I was destroyed, devastated.

"No, Mama," I pleaded, trembling. "That's not true! I love you!"

"Well, I don't love you!" she shrieked as she grabbed me and shook me furiously. Her long, sharp fingernails ripped into my skin. "You are a curse on us! I hate you."

"Mama!" I cried louder. "You're hurting me!"

Then in front of a crowd of mediums who had gathered at our house to drink coffee, she denounced her little boy in a demonic sing-song. "No, you're not mine, not mine! Hand of Lucifer is upon his life... finger of Satan, touch his life... finger of Satan, touch his soul... mark of the beast on his heart. No, not my son, not mine!"

Suddenly various demonic voices began to speak through her, some masculine, some feminine. "You are the son of Satan!" they screeched, mocking me. "Get out. Go out of this house! You are not welcome here."

"No, no, Mama," I wept.

"I hate you," she spat. "You are not any son of mine. You are the devil's son, sent here to destroy us. I hate you, I hate you, I hate you."

That was my last day as an innocent little boy. I fled from the house, weeping, and hid in the dust under our house, covering myself with dirt. My father sought me out that night, but I ran away and hid in the forest for several nights, accompanied only by the parrots and the fireflies and the singing tree frogs. I swam in the cool brooks and watched the big fish.

And emotionally, I shriveled up until I was unable to care about anything or anybody except my own survival.

I never cried again during my childhood. My tears dried up and my heart hardened into stone. I returned home several mornings later, defiant; but from then on my mother and I became increasingly spiteful enemies. I needed her love—but at the same time I swore that I hated her and would someday kill her.

FLY AWAY, LITTLE BIRD

One of the most precious memories I have of my father would also become one of the most painful. I was about five years old at the time, and this incident represents the one and only occasion I can recall that my father ever showed me any affection.

One evening when the cool breezes swept off the ocean onto our porch, Papa took me to himself, pipe held firmly in his mouth. It was evening and the mountains were so close you felt you could

A Lonely Saturday Afternoon

I never had a childhood and I didn't expect to have a future. I had no clue what happiness was all about. It was a Saturday afternoon in late spring and I was feeling extremely sad and lonely. I left my little apartment and went to Prospect Park, which divides Brooklyn from Flatbush. I had just been in a violent rumble the night before and had severely hurt three or four of the other gang's members. I had used my gun and knife, shooting and cutting people.

I was walking through the park with my hands in my pockets when I noticed a family together. They had obviously come out to spend the day in the park. I saw a father with his son. He was tossing his son up in the air, chasing him around their blanket, hugging and kissing him.

Suddenly I was seized with hatred for that man and his son. I hated the man and I hated the kid with everything in my deeply scarred soul. I had always, subconsciously, yearned for a relationship like that. The little boy didn't even realize how fortunate he was to have someone who loved him. Unable to control my anger, I strode over to them, spat on them, and started cursing them out with every profane word I knew. Demonic hatred spewed out of my mouth and covered them in filth.

Why was I so angry? Because I envied those parents, playing with their kids. They reminded me that I had been cheated out of the hugs of a father, the kisses of a mother. I felt this void most deeply on Saturdays, because that was the day I felt most abandoned. Nothing was going on. My gang friends weren't around. I knew that later I would go back to my empty apartment and try to sleep, but the only sound I'd hear might be the barking of a dog in the midnight hours—the loneliest sound on earth. I would be truly alone... again. And so to see a happy family playing in the park was just too much. I cursed them for having what I always wanted but could never have. I didn't know it, but I was starving for love and for a childhood that I never enjoyed.

reach out and embrace them. Papa told me about a bird that had become a legend in Puerto Rico. This bird had no legs and was condemned to stay aloft continually. I was captivated by his story; it challenged the castle of my imagination. I was happy for the bird. I wanted him to make it. But several questions troubled me.

"Papa, how did the bird eat?"

"The little bird floated with the currents and fed on the insects riding the wind," he told me.

Then another question occurred to me.

"Papa—what happens when the little bird comes down?"

"The only time he ever stops flying—the only time he comes to earth—is when he dies. For once he touches the earth, he can never run again," he replied as he sat rocking in his chair on the veranda, smoking his pipe.

As a child you remember things—like a fire in your mind. That's what this story became for me, a fire in my mind. I continued to think about it even as my home situation deteriorated over the next ten years.

Finally, when I was fifteen years old, my father took me to the airport, gave me a ten-dollar bill, handed a plane ticket to the attendant and put me on a plane to New York. "Be a good boy, little bird," he said to me.

The words hit me like a blow to the stomach. I knew my father was telling me in his own way that I would never see him again. There was no hope for me. I was a legless little bird who couldn't stay aloft forever. One day soon, my father was saying, I would come down. And I'd never fly again.

There's no hope for you, a voice whispered down deep in my soul.

Once in New York I quickly became part of a vicious bunch of street hoods called the Mau Maus. They stole whatever they wanted and were no strangers to burglary, extortion, intimidation, and even armed robbery. Yet they became my family. I fought my way to the top through sheer brutality. It was a brutal city and I figured I had to be tougher than anyone if I was to be king of the streets, lord of the concrete jungle. So I became meaner than everyone; I survived when others died.

At least that much about the gangs hasn't changed. They *seem* to provide the love and acceptance that children do not receive in their own homes—but the price is life itself. Literally, in far too many cases.

NEEDED: LOVING DISCIPLINE

If we want to keep our own children out of the gangs and uninvolved with the violence that's sweeping our cities and our schools, the main question we have to ask ourselves is how can we create an environment in which our children feel loved? How can we display our love to our children?

I believe that it's in the first ten years of life that you can have the greatest influence on a child. We need to teach our kids the way of God, respect for their neighbors, and the value of education. We show them we love them by reading the Bible with them, by praying with them. We show them love by supervising what kind of people they hang around.

If we don't break our kids of these habits in the beginning, they're going to break us in the end. There's no way to replace love with the giving of trinkets—stereos, clothes, cars, whatever. We've got to give of ourselves physically, morally, and spiritually. We've got to let our kids know that we can be hurt; we've got to show them the soft underbelly of our life. Then they'll know that we're real and that our love is for real.

Our nation is in a Great Depression—of love. There is little anymore that holds our nation together except our fragile economy. What would happen if that economy should collapse? Unless things change, families won't be there to hold together the jagged pieces. This nation will shatter like a worn-out porcelain jar hitting a cement floor. To have a strong nation we need strong families.

Even though as a father I was absent during the weekends when most families bond together as they retire from school and work and the weekly routines, somehow, with God's help, Sunday school, and the Bible, our children developed a strong sense of family. We were definitely different from the other families. But we managed to convey that the purpose of my traveling was to help people. Others needed to know about Jesus! Our children knew a little about my background, even though I didn't let them read *Run, Baby, Run* until they were twelve years old. We owed everything to Jesus, who changed both my life and Gloria's.

It is past time that we bring back *fatherhood* to the neighborhoods. Selfishness is too expensive; sacrifice is necessary. Men must be fathers to these kids.

I know we do have a lot of fathers in this country who love their kids enough to die for them. I'm not suggesting that all fathers have shirked their responsibilities. But many of us need to abandon the macho attitude that refuses to allow our kids to see us tender and sweet. We fathers need to be sensitive, to show our kids love

---

Life in the War Zone

Recent studies have investigated the effects of growing up surrounded by violence. Many of them conclude that children of the inner city behave and live in ways startlingly like children living in war zones. They "quickly adapt to their hazardous surroundings in ways that seem shocking to outsiders. They regularly see friends and relatives die simply because they are in the wrong place—the path of a bullet—at the wrong time."[S1]

Author James Garbarino, president of the Erikson Institute for Advanced Study in Child Development in Chicago, has studied children and violence for many years. In his book, *No Place to Be a Child*, he describes what happens to the minds of children who are exposed to constant violence in areas around the world (places such as Cambodia, the Mideast—and inner-city Chicago). He sees many startling similarities between the Chicago projects and Cambodian refugee camps: Guns are plentiful, inconsequential arguments end in violence, adult males are seldom around, mothers are often clinically depressed. In both places, he says, young boys not even in their late teens already have become soldiers. In Cambodia, they are guerrilla fighters; in Chicago, they are gang members.[S2]

continued on facing page

through hugs and kisses. Our children need to see tenderness from their fathers.

I know a lot of young men today in their late teens or early twenties who still identify their fathers as their heroes. They don't name sports heroes or movie idols; they single out their dads. That's what I'm calling for today, dads who set out to be their children's heroes.

Now, I know it is unlikely that you are a resident of an inner-city ghetto. But I know of far too many homes that look good on the outside but are rotten inside. My friend Bobby Cruz recently told me of an incident in his hometown of Miami. One day he received a call to help a cousin whose son was deeply into drugs. When Bobby went to the house, he couldn't help but notice the expensive home and elegant neighborhood. In the driveway he saw a $50,000 car loaded with every option imaginable—cellular phone, CD player,

---

Garbarino claims that post-traumatic stress disorder (PTSD), a condition usually suffered by war veterans, is common also among children who grow up with violence. But this shouldn't surprise us. Bullets whizzing by in the city are no different from bullets whizzing by on the battlefield. The bodies are just as real. So is the blood. Why should it surprise us if human beings react the same way to one firefight as they do to another?

Still, differences certainly do exist between children of war and children of the inner city. Garbarino says that inner-city youths *may have the rougher time.* They probably suffer from lifelong poor nutrition, have substandard educations, and few employment opportunities. Children in war zones "are much more likely to have a couple of domains of their life still be intact," while children in the inner cities likely come from situations where family structures have been destroyed, perhaps for generations.[53]

I look at all of this through the grid of my own life. We forget that there is something inside these children that we have to touch. They're crying out to us that they are hurting, that they are suffering. They're asking for a miracle, the gift of life. Some are asking whether life is even worth the effort. Life is that traumatic.

outrageous sound system. Then my friend found out it belonged to his cousin's fourteen-year-old kid—the one who wasn't yet old enough to drive legally and who was having the severe drug problems that prompted the call to Bobby in the first place. Somehow this boy's parents couldn't see that they were the ones helping to destroy their son.

Let me tell you, indulgence is not loving. In the long run, it's just as much a soul-killer as abuse. Remember the comments by the officers at the beginning of this chapter? Just a few years ago, the only kids interested in joining the gangs were from dysfunctional, economically impoverished, inner-city homes. No more. Now kids from middle- and upper-class homes are joining the gangs. As a show of rebellion, the officers said. Rebellion against what? Against homes that try to buy them off. Against parents who mistake lots of trinkets for lots of love.

Giving in to kids can be a parent's biggest mistake. In homes without loving discipline, kids become experts at wrapping parents around their little fingers. Being too lenient is the kiss of death.

If we do this, in the long run our kids will hold us hostage. Yet if we had disciplined them in love in the beginning, it wouldn't have happened. Conflict is not pleasant, but it's often necessary. Like they say, you can pay now, or you can pay later.

What's lacking in too many of our homes is a true, vital masculine presence, not macho brutality. Appropriate discipline shows a child he or she is truly loved. And that kind of love can keep kids from the gangs.

What hurts us so severely in this country is the acute lack of caring parenthood, especially the absence of fathers and a strong image of a father. That's what is killing the spirit of America.

HEROES IN SHORT SUPPLY

Some way, somehow, our children must once more begin to look to their parents as their biggest heroes. We must be the kind of people who represent what is respectable. We must love them, care for them, discipline them, provide for them. They must begin to see us not only as good fathers and mothers, but as good human beings.

When children once more begin to look at their fathers as the biggest heroes they know, we can reverse the appalling decline of this country. *Nobody* can replace the family or a father. Intact families represent the ultimate earthly love. There is a divine love and a physical love, and the highest physical love possible is found only in the family.

Too much leniency and our kids rebel. Opt for brutality and we will put our children into depression and despair, questioning why they are even here. I know it is simplistic to say the answer is love, but sometimes simplistic answers are true. Two plus two equals four—simple, but true. If we want to put this country back on course to sanity and health, it is going to take mothers and fathers who take their roles seriously, who commit themselves wholeheartedly to the Lord Jesus in love.

There are practical ways to show this love and spread this love beyond the four walls of our own homes, and we'll talk about some of those later in this book. But for now, as a father myself, I want to challenge you to recommit yourself to loving your children and letting them know that they will always have a special place in the depths of your heart. Violence really doesn't drop out of the sky into teenagers when they become fifteen; it begins when eight-year-olds are denied the love of their parents which they so desperately need.

I grew up in a very abusive home and those ugly experiences are still very much in my mind. Time has not dulled my memories of being labeled ugly, stupid, a child who had no business being in this world. We must be extraordinarily careful about the vocabulary we use with our kids.

In the heat of the moment, we must take care not to lose track of what our mouths are telling our kids. We don't know what words will remain forever in those little minds. I believe every child is hungry to be complimented by his or her father. They are dying to hear their dads say, "You are so special! I am so proud of you, of what you have accomplished. You have done a great job!" A kid hears that and he's on cloud nine. Sure, we have to correct when needed and give good advice, but we can never forget how important fatherly compliments are. Money can never buy what a single "I'm so proud of you" can accomplish in a child's life. I know of many adults who have long since left their parents' homes, but even today they long for a dad or a mom to say something positive about them. Many parents feel uncomfortable expressing pride in their adult kids, but they have to do it. It's priceless.

I wonder: Do your own kids know how much you love them? Or is a gang even now whispering in their ears?

"IF GOD IS LIKE MY FATHER, I DON'T WANT NO GOD"

I will never forget my 1994 crusade in Houston. Our meetings were jam-packed. People were everywhere, hungry for the message of Jesus' love and acceptance. When I gave the altar call, scores of women and children—and men in particular—were coming from all parts of the facility.

The Drug Connection

Much, perhaps most, of today's youth violence is spawned by drug use. Today's drug scene is a powerful soul-killer of our youth, and the current scene is a far cry even from what it was just a few years ago. Marijuana produced today is multiple times more potent than that smoked by the hippies of the free-love sixties. Heroin is several *hundred* times more lethal. In addition to those well-known street poisons, kids have available to them all manner of cocaine, psychedelic drugs (a more powerful LSD is making a big comeback), crack, ice, ecstasy, PCP, and constantly changing "designer drugs."

Who is the target market for this poison? Kids ages eight to seventeen. More than seventy-nine thousand kids are on crack in New York City alone. It's not hard at all to understand why boys and girls are dropping out of school in New York at ever-increasing rates. Everybody knows that there's more money in drugs than in fast food. Why slave several hours a day over a greasy griddle for $4.25 an hour if you can make five hundred to one thousand dollars a day selling drugs?

continued on facing page

It's interesting, but most of the people who accept Christ at my crusades are men. That's true all over the world. That night in Houston, I was so touched that the men present identified with the masculine image I tried to portray. I told them how a supernatural experience with Christ had changed me in a miraculous way and made me a real man. When I came to know Jesus, I became truly masculine for the first time. I gave up my macho counterfeit and began to learn what things were good and which were bad, and to pursue the good things. I began to take responsibility for my actions. I told them that Jesus is 100 percent human and 100 percent divine, and he is a man's man. He showed his muscle in many thrilling ways, by changing people through supernatural displays of power and love. My message that night resonated with the crowd, especially with the men.

That probably explains why I noticed Jamie. She stood out. She

The diabolic power of drugs that comes into the heart, soul, and spirit of a person damages and poisons the essence of what he or she is: God's creation. The United States has become a land of betrayal. Espionage is not the only type of treachery that can destroy a country from within. People have slowly come to accept violence and drugs in this country. The United States has copped out in so many areas, with our live-and-let-live attitude, always cautious of stepping on anybody's personal freedoms. Since no one seems to have an answer for the drug problem, we accept drugs as a part of our society. We have lost the strength to deal with this issue that seems hopeless. Without the moral courage to confront these problems, we are betraying not only ourselves but the future of our children.

I have come to the conclusion that drug abuse is a demon from hell. It's an attractive evil. We might not be able to kill the demon, but we must go after its victims. This is the time of deliverance. Evangelical or not, conservative or not, we must unite to deliver our children from the clutches of this great evil. They must be delivered out of slavery into sweet freedom. We need another Moses!

was about fifteen years old, and when I gave the altar call, she came down and stood right in front of me. I could tell from her cold expression that she was very stubborn and hard. It wasn't difficult to see that she was present through someone else's choice. She wasn't interested in listening to some evangelist talk about Jesus.

I found out later that her mother had insisted she come to the crusade. But now, as I watched her, she broke my heart. I noticed that regardless of how many people were praying for her, she remained cold, aloof, disdainful. As I continued to look, I saw a sad story written all over her angry face. Two black eyes and numerous small cuts marred her face, as if she had been beaten up. Soon I decided to approach her. I just looked at her for a while. Finally I said, "Your father beat you up." That came to me right away; I didn't say "your mom" or "your brother" or "your boyfriend" or "some gang members." "Your father beat you up," I repeated. "Yes," she replied, almost choking with anger. You could feel both the hurt and the hate welling up inside her. "Yes, my father beat me up unmercifully—and he is a Christian," she said accusingly.

I later discovered that she meant her father attended church once in a while. But at that moment, her statement tore me up. This man had left very heavy scars on his little girl, and she quickly learned to connect his evil actions with God himself. It was clear these cuts and bruises didn't represent the first such attack either. It was very difficult to talk to Jamie until I said, "You don't mind if I pray for you? You're not going to reject the prayer?" She looked at me and said meekly, "No, you can pray for me." Then she broke down and wept.

As hard as the whole conversation was, what bothered me the most was a statement she made at the beginning of our talk. "You know," she said, "look what my father has done to me. Look at the way he has treated me for such a long time. If God is like my father, I don't want no God. I don't want him. He's ugly. He's brutal. He's just up there, not to love you, but to club you with a baseball bat. I don't want him. If God is like my father, I don't want no God."

I'm very happy to say that I tried to show Jamie that night that

God acts nothing like her earthly father. I was able to show her that God loves her so much, in fact, that he sent his only Son to die on her behalf, to take the full punishment for her sins, the same punishment we all deserve. And God doesn't own a baseball bat! That's a lie of the devil. God's heart breaks when innocent people are abused and mistreated, and he reaches out to them in infinite love and acceptance. That was the message I was privileged to deliver to Jamie that night, and she began to believe it.

That ultimately is the only message with enough power to reshape America. The love of God and the gospel of Jesus Christ is the only message that can take the hate out of a gang member's heart and replace it with love. It's the only message that can heal a broken heart like Jamie's. In fact, I can say without a shred of doubt that America's epidemic of youth violence has only one answer: God himself.

My wife Gloria has been visiting the Zebulon Pike Detention Center in our hometown for the past fifteen years, ministering to the kids there. She says, "The boys' faces gleam as I tell them, 'You are men, the head of your future families. Only you can break the cycle of violence, alcohol, and drugs in your families. Jesus understands your fears, problems, even your hate! Doctor Jesus wants to heal your broken hearts, dreams, and lives. His love can change your lives now! He forgives and forgets—forever—our past sins, our present sins, even our future sins. What a good God! You *can* start over. This is the bottom line of Christianity: Never give up, not on yourselves or on life."

We have also established a family tradition of visiting Zeb Pike on Christmas Day. We sing songs, hand out presents, and pray for the kids. I speak to them about my past and tell them about Jesus' love for them.

We see many of these kids after they get released. We run into them all over the city, in grocery stores, in malls, and restaurants, those who have attended Gloria's Bible studies at Zeb Pike. Some of them are now adults, some have really straightened out their lives, while others avoid her because they are still involved in the same illegal activities. It has been a hard fight, but my wife loves it.

I was at a hamburger stand recently when a young girl behind the counter said, "Hi, Mr. Cruz. Remember me?" Noting my inquisitive look, the girl whispered, "Zeb Pike." The other day at the car wash a young man approached me and said, "Hey, do you still go to Zeb Pike?" After explaining that he was there a couple of years ago during a Christmas visit, he said, "Your wife prayed for me as I gave my life to Jesus in one of her Bible studies at the detention home. She helped me a lot."

I love to use the family as an example. It shows how family members can make a difference in our communities. You don't have to hold a crusade for thousands of people to be used by God. Jesus calls each of us to evangelize and bear fruit. The only thing that will last for eternity are people. Nothing else—not cars, buildings, church facilities, money, or houses—will endure.

God really is the only answer for America. I'm sure that doesn't surprise you, coming from an evangelist—but would you be surprised to hear that many gang members still respect God? They may be contemptuous of every human authority and scornful of religious phonies, but the gang members I talk to around the country still have a respect for God.

That's crucial to remember as we wind down the first part of this book. Don't you dare begin to think that our problems have no solutions. Don't you dare imagine that our cities are without hope! Our God is the God of hope. And I want to show you just a little of that tremendous hope in the next chapter.

CHAPTER 4

R-E-S-P-E-C-T

You may not believe it, but many gang members still have a healthy respect for God. There still is a small part of them that belongs to God, and I'm going to find it and go after it.

A couple of months ago I visited Victory Outreach Ministries in La Puente, California, to meet with four young men—two of them former gang members turned Christians, two of them still in the gangs.

We sat in a semicircle flanked by a table stocked with fruit, beverages, and assorted munchies, kindly provided by the church. The plain Sunday school room where we met was deserted except for the four young men, myself, a church volunteer, and another friend. I made it clear as we began that I wasn't there to judge anyone, but that I wanted to hear straight from their hearts what it was like to be in gangs today. Two of the young men had been members of the Bassett Grande gang; the two others belonged to one of the sixty-nine East L.A. gangs.

None of the four—Johnnie, twenty-two; Tommy, nineteen; Ernie, eighteen; or Alex, eighteen—would look me straight in the eye at the beginning. They sat slouched in their metal chairs, gazing most of the time at a vague spot on the floor. A couple wore beepers, just in case a "business deal" were to call them away. Crude tattoos were etched into their arms, testifying to their particular gang affiliation. At first they were extremely reluctant to speak, perhaps trying to make up their minds whether I was someone who could be trusted.

To help encourage open conversation, I told them a little of my own history in the gangs. I explained how I had climbed to the top of a vicious New York gang by sheer brutality, how I had done my own share of shooting, stabbing, robbing. But that was behind me now. Now I wanted to help those who were in the gangs, and they could help me do that by telling me what life was like for them.

As they warmed to me and began to open up, our conversation ranged over several topics. Ernie confessed he made a little money hustling, and when asked he said he didn't have a hero. All four came from families with longtime gang roots; some had been addicted to drugs, others stayed away from them. One admitted that the sight of blood "haunted" him, while another claimed that AK-47s, nine-millimeter automatic pistols, and grenades were the weapons of choice these days. ("Thirty-eights ain't nothin' no more," he said.) We talked about school, about family, about gang initiations. But mostly, I wanted to know what they thought about God.

I want you to hear what these four young men had to say about a gang member's respect for God. Then ask yourself this question: Is there any hope for the young people trapped in the dead-end lifestyle of the gangs? Or should we just give up?

Nicky: What do you think about Jesus Christ? About God? Do you respect him?

Alex: I don't know much about him.

Nicky: But do you respect him?

Alex: I ain't gonna say I do 'cause I don't know. But I have respect, I mean, I have tried to respect him. When I remember him—I'll just kick it, and not do what I was going to do.

Nicky: If somebody came to you to talk to you about Jesus, would you respect him?

Alex: I respect that person, sure. I always respect that person.

Nicky: Do you think that the gangs have that sense of respect for God? What happens when one of your guys gets converted to Jesus, and he says, "I'm clean"?

Alex: I do respect him, but I'm not ready to explore it myself. I know there is one who could help a lot, but...

Johnny: There's some, they got the attitude. You try to share the Word with them and they're, "Oh, I don't need that," and this and that. But deep down inside, they really want it. They're crying out for that help. That's how I was, you know. But if the homeboys are there, they want to put up that front.

Nicky: Do you feel that you have hope now?

Johnny: When I was out there, when I was caught up in the gang, I had no sense of direction. There came times, if I would have had the guts to do it, I would have blown my brains out. But I didn't have the guts to do that—that's how lost I was. That's how much the devil had me bound. The violence, the things that I had done. I just got out of prison a few months ago, praise God that I did. But now—I still have my tattoos and whatever, but I have a sense of direction. I know where I'm going and I could care less what people think about me now. They might look at me and judge me from my outer appearance, but now, praise God, I know there is hope and I have it. My wife is a born-again Christian too. Everything is right now: I've got my kids, I can be the person I've always wanted to be.

Nicky: Do you feel good that you've got people around you now, Christian friends?

Johnny: I like it, you know? I still have a lot of love for my homeboys and my neighborhood....

Nicky: Well, you don't want to lose that; sure, you still have that. I still love my old friends, but now I love them differently. I want them to change.

Johnny: When you're caught up like that, you want a way out, but you can't see how to do it. I see homeboys who try to leave, they try to get married, but they always find themselves back in the neighborhood. And they're never happy. They try to get a job, but that doesn't work. They try different things, but that never seems to work. They might even try to get out of the gang, and later on a rival might see them or recognize them, and say, "He ain't getting away." He might not be from that gang anymore, but his rival says, "He shot me or killed my homeboy," or whatever, and they're going to deal with him.

Nicky: Your homeboy, your homegirl, your 'hood—when you approach them and they say, "What's up?" and they think you're still smoking marijuana or crack or you're doing something illegal for the gang but you tell them you're not—what would be the reaction?

Tommy: Sometimes you tell them, "I just quit," but they say, "You can't just quit." I know what got me out—Jesus Christ. My homeboys, they'll check up on the church, you know, to make sure I'm for real. I just saw some of them the other day, and I was talking to them and they straight up pulled a knife on me. I told them, "I'm not going to die for you." I told them, "You can do whatever you want to me, but I'm not going to go back."

Nicky: Yes, that's the respect I meant. The black gangs are the same way. You come back around and they check you out. They're checking you out because they want to know if you're for real or if you're a phony.

Tommy: Before it happened constantly, but now it's rare.

Nicky: So they respect you, they don't bother you anymore?

Tommy: Yeah. Some of them even come to the church.

Nicky: What about you?

Johnny: My homeboys respect what I'm doing. I see it as, when I was there, I did what I had to do. To me, my answer is, I could care less what they think. You know what I'm saying? I could care less what they think. They know me, I got my respect in my neighborhood, in my family. Even when I was out there caught up in the world, my own homeboys used to tell me, "Why don't you just kick back already, slow down?" Now that I'm doing what I'm doing, I know they respect me for it. What I'm trying to do now is set a good example for them, to let them know there's a way out of it.

Nicky: What about you, sir? After listening to this guy over here?

Johnny: He's from my neighborhood; we're from the same gang.

Nicky: What about you, sir?

Ernie: Like you say, I respect God and everything. My mom, she's been saved for a while....

Nicky: She's a Christian?

Ernie: Yeah. Going on ten years, I guess. I think the only reason I made it through so far is her. You know?

Nicky: You give credit in some way to God?

Ernie: Yeah, I look back and there's times when I got lucky. I got a bullet hole in my door to prove it, you know?

Nicky: So there's no guarantee that you might come home? You might go out and you don't know what's coming your way.

Ernie: Yeah.

Nicky: So your mother has been there for you. That's the reason so many kids today are leaving the gangs, because they have a praying mother or a praying father. And God answers their prayers.

After our conversation had run its course and we were getting ready to leave, I wanted to find out where one of the young men stood with God. When I told him that I respected both his intelligence and his courage, his eyes lit up; it was clear few adults had ever talked to him like that. I asked him if he knew that God loved him, just as he was, and that he wanted to give him a new life full of hope and meaning. He had heard it before, he said, but he wasn't sure it was for him just yet. He was clearly uncomfortable, yet he just as clearly wanted to know more about how an outsider like me could see such potential in him.

He was like a hungry salmon circling a tasty morsel thrashing about in front of his eyes, yet refusing to strike for fear that some string might come attached, complete with barbed hook. He reminded me of C.S. Lewis' words about our unwillingness to believe in the staggering generosity of God. "We are half-hearted creatures," Lewis wrote, "fooling about with drink and sex and ambition when infinite joy is offered us, like an ignorant child who wants to go on making mud pies in a slum because he cannot imagine what is meant by the offer of a holiday at the sea."[1]

This young man didn't come to faith that day, but he's willing to listen. *And that's our area of opportunity with the gangs.* They still

Times Have Changed

When I was in the gangs, we lived by a strict code: love, faithfulness, loyalty, honor. Most gangs today have nothing like this. Yet if you compared them with us on a level playing field, the gangs today wouldn't stand a chance. In that day we operated with a sense of intelligence and toughness. We were more healthy in our minds; we didn't allow drugs to destroy us as they are destroying today's gang members. In fact, we wouldn't allow an addict to join the gang, since he would be a liability. We needed people who would be quick on their feet and agile in their minds. Once a guy started using drugs, we didn't want him. He could jeopardize us because he wasn't strong.

Our enemies were clear-cut: the law, other gangs, and those who transgressed our turf. We didn't allow our members to rape or to attack innocent bystanders. We protected the elderly people within our turf; we didn't allow anyone to be disrespectful to them or attack them. They were the grandparents of our neighborhood.

I don't mean to suggest that we were saints. We weren't! We were mean and brutal, the Dracula of the night. We slept by day and prowled the neighborhood by night. But there were other major differences between then and now. For example, we settled differences between gangs in a formalized way. Gang leaders convened a war concert, where they went with bodyguards to decide where to have the next "rumble." We'd set the time, the place and what kind of weapons that would be used. Even back then we had automatic pistols and shotguns—but today the gangs regularly use AK-47s, Uzi submachine guns, and even heavier weapons. It's like the Old West—without rules, without morals, barbaric.

Our primary aim was to protect our turf, our neighborhood. After all, that's where we lived. We weren't allowed to sell drugs to

continued on facing page

have a real respect for God. The average Christian or the average media reporter doesn't understand that. They see angry, violent gang members and convince themselves that these young people are beyond hope. But they aren't.

Many of the gangs are fair. When they see a change in one of

---

another member of the gang. You absolutely could not betray your homeboy. You couldn't rat on someone—"rat" was the lowest thing you could call someone.

We never had drive-by shootings. We would have considered that "chicken." We were the pioneers, who fought with skill and cunning. We were classic street fighters. The last thing we ever did was to attack a family. We only did so when members of that family were withholding information that we needed.

When Hector, a fellow Mau Mau, tied up his uncle and beat him, I went after him. We didn't like the way he gave his uncle no chance to defend himself. I laid into him and then he challenged me in front of the gang. "Let's go to the park and settle this," he said to me. "Whatever weapon you want," I replied. He chose the switchblade.

So about 11 P.M. we walked to the park alone to settle it. That meant one of us was about to die. I was wearing my leather jacket, since it was almost winter and already was very cold. The park was about a quarter of a mile away, and I used the time it took to walk that distance to plan how I was going to take Hector out. I figured I would wrap my jacket around my arm, let him attack, then go for his gut with my blade in my other hand.

It was very dark when we got to the park. I could hear Hector breathing heavily—out of fear, I knew. "Come on," I challenged him, "try to do to me what you did to your uncle."

There was a pause, and then Hector said, "Nicky, you're my friend, my brother. Why do we have to fight? We're going to destroy each other."

I wasn't eager for the fight either, so we called it off. Later Hector killed two guys and was sent to the penitentiary in Puerto Rico. He's still there. I visited him once to tell him about the life available in Jesus, but he didn't respond at that time. Maybe his time is coming.

their members who has given his life to God, they extend a certain lenience to that member. They're not afraid that person is going to rat on them or be a chicken. But they will watch that member to see if the claimed conversion is real, to see if he is what he says he is. Has he really changed?

Imagine two different scenarios. In one of them, a new convert walks up to one of his homeboys and says, "What's up, dude?"

"Not too much."

"Well, I just gave my life to Jesus Christ and I came over here to tell you about him. I'm not going banging anymore; I'm not fooling around with drugs. I'm going to church."

That gang member is going to be surprised, he may ridicule his friend, but if he sees the conversion is real, he'll respect that friend. But imagine another conversation between the same two people.

"What's up, dude?"

"Not too much."

"Hey, do you have some weed or anything? PCP?"

That person not only won't have a testimony for Jesus, the gang won't trust him; he isn't worth anything to them. If a new convert can mingle with his old homeboys and not compromise his new convictions, however, there is a strong possibility his homeboys may one day come with him to church. If these young men and women show the goods—that they love Jesus—the possibility is great that they will succeed in bringing many gang members to the Lord.

That's why I encourage upper-middle-class churches to invest heavily in the ministry of churches like Victory Outreach. Why? Because if anyone is going to have a ministry in the life of the gangs, it's churches made up in large part of former gang members. Welfare didn't work in cleaning up the inner cities, but a church concentrating on strong evangelism in the heart of the nation's war zones will. I am living proof that Christ has the power to change the hearts of violent gang members. The church wasn't sure how to bring my gang buddies to the Lord, but as a former gang member, I was. We need to encourage these effective soul-winning inner-city churches by helping them get the resources they need to be effective. Maybe you can't effectively reach a gang member; but there's an inner-city church that could, if it just had the resources. Maybe it's your part to help provide them!

HOPE THAT TRANSFORMS

God has privileged me to give hope to many inner-city kids. They see me and hear my story and they tell themselves, "He changed; I can change, too." But my change didn't happen overnight. I fought being Latin, I fought a minority accent. I fought a lack of social skills and manners. I fought myself—the painful memories I had carried with me for years. My background haunted me. But I too had a sense of pride in competing with the best of the best. The family of the Lord is one of the greatest families ever. They are there for you. The great satisfaction is to overcome all the strikes against you. But my goal was heaven. I strongly believe that where there's a will, there's a way—and that will was given to me by Christ to overcome all things.

I tell everyone that it took a supernatural miracle to change my life, to really turn me around from my wicked ways, to leave my gang and give up the drugs and the violence. I was fighting against everything. I became a survivor and I acknowledged the miracle that God did in my life. And I tell whoever will listen that God can do the same for them. Miracles can happen if you turn your church loose.

I'm thinking right now of several gang members who came to the Lord in a Houston crusade back in 1991. Since then, some dramatic events have taken place in their lives. Let me tell you about three of them.

Alberto came to a church meeting with his mom. This kid had five faces tattooed on his arm, plus the face of the devil. The five human faces were those of his best friends, all of whom had been killed in the previous six months. That night I preached about violence in the United States, about kids starving for love. I spoke a little about my own life and hundreds of people came forward to the altar afterward. For over an hour people kept coming up to talk with me and to get my photograph or autograph.

Finally a church deacon approached me and said some kid really wanted to talk to me. "He's in the gangs," the deacon told me. When Alberto walked up, I said, "Let's go someplace private," so we were taken to the pastor's study.

When I looked into Alberto's eyes I saw a deeply troubled young man. Loneliness and anger were burning fiercely behind his mask of

Legion Is Their Name

I honestly feel that if you look at New York City and Los Angeles and many other cities across this nation, evil spirits have gotten into the skins of our kids; the pain is in them and it's killing them. They are not at all unlike the demon-possessed man of Mark 5:1-20.

Do you remember the story? Jesus and his disciples sailed across the Sea of Galilee to the country of the Gerasenes. As soon as Jesus got out of the boat, a demon-possessed man ran from the tombs to meet him. Mark says:

> This man lived in the tombs, and no one could bind him any more, not even with a chain. For he had often been chained hand and foot, but he tore the chains apart and broke the irons on his feet. No one was strong enough to subdue him. Night and day among the tombs and in the hills he would cry out and cut himself with stones.   **Mark 5:3-5**

After a short, supernatural encounter with Jesus, the man—who had called himself "Legion, for we are many"—was freed of the evil spirits. Jesus commanded the demons to leave the man and allowed them to enter into a herd of pigs nearby, which went crazy and ran into the lake and drowned. When the locals heard the strange reports, they came to Jesus and found this man "sitting there, dressed and in his right mind" (Mk 5:15). It frightened them so badly they asked Jesus to leave!

I believe that demon-possessed man is like the gangs today. He had no recollections about his family. Nobody knew where he came from. Did he have family? Friends? Children? What interrupted his life? We don't know. We do know that he became vulner-

continued on facing page

toughness. I thought at first he wanted an autograph, but I quickly discovered he really wanted to talk.

"How are you doing?" I asked.

"I'm in trouble," he replied—and then, out of the clear blue sky, the Holy Spirit prompted me to reach out to him, put my arm around him and say, "Come over here, son. You're starving for

able, evil sunk its hooks into him, and he created a huge problem for society.

The man gave up on the good life, became homeless, and chose death and the cemetery to be his new residence. He was hopeless, helpless, and controlled by an invisible, evil force which held captive the castle of his imagination. His mind was quickly conquered by these wicked spirits. He wouldn't know even if he had a father, a mother, brothers, or sisters, whether he was married or had children. His mind was fried; he was gone.

The man was "treated" by government officials, community activists, social workers, psychologists, psychiatrists of his time—but they were all powerless. None of them could do a thing. So they grew fearful of him and abandoned him to his lonely and wretched fate.

The "church" of his day (the Pharisees) was heavily involved in fasting and public prayer—yet it couldn't hear the voice of the man from the cemetery. How could it? It wasn't even listening. As far as the Pharisees were concerned, he was dead already.

I hate to admit it, but this man is still with us today. He is the very picture of what's happening right now to our youth.

Just as in his day, fear and intimidation have tied the hands of the professionals. We have been completely frozen by how the drug culture has moved into our neighborhoods. It has many names—they are Legion—and it destroys the minds of our children and their families. And just like the demon-possessed man, we have grown afraid of it. Nobody seems able to help. We find ourselves dealing with drug addictions and violence that destroy the heart and mind and body and spirit of a person just as surely as does demon possesssion—and we seem handcuffed to do do anything about it.

Who can help? Only Jesus!

love." I'd never done that in my entire ministry!

Well, it was too much. Alberto immediately broke down in deep, anguished sobs. He started moaning and groaning like a little boy lost in the desert.

"What you really need is to be loved by Jesus," I told him. "Do you want to love him?"

"Yes," was all he could say.

I led him to faith in Christ right there in that little room, then I asked him where his parents were.

"My mother's here," he said slowly, "but I beat her up pretty bad."

"What?" I demanded. "You're telling me that you beat her up?"

"Yes, sir," he said meekly.

Right then I took authority as his father. "I want you to go get your mother and bring her here right now," I ordered.

"Yes, sir," he replied.

A few minutes later he reappeared with his mother. She was cut and bruised all over. I told him to apologize to his mother, which he promptly did. I then told him to give her a big hug and thank her for loving him enough to bring him to the meeting, which he also did promptly. Finally I grabbed both of them and wrapped them in a big bear hug. Both of them were crying and rejoicing at the same time.

That kid went home and reached his whole family for Jesus. I'm still in contact with him, and he's still doing fantastic.

Another gang member, Fernando, had been going to church for some time prior to the crusade. He had been a gang leader and was in a great personal battle whether to go back to the gangs. Fernando had spent the summer of 1989 at a Christian camp and it was there that God began to deal with him about his life. Yet it was not until the night of the crusade, when he saw the power of the gospel, that he was completely set free and was called to be a minister of the Good News. That night, it was Fernando who was responsible for bringing many other gang leaders who gave their lives to Christ. Fernando is now working with the youth group of that church, Iglesia Sobre la Roca (Church on the Rock).

The third young man is Adrian. He was the gang leader of a group called the 752s. During one of our crusades in May of 1990, Adrian gave his life to Christ at a service at Iglesia Sobre la Roca, along with four other gang leaders.

Adrian was a stud, really. He was a vicious fighter and everyone was afraid of him. He had never been in a church until a former gang member brought him. I was giving my testimony and as I began to describe my family background, Adrian began sweating and shaking. Finally he rushed out of the auditorium and into the bathroom, where he began throwing up. Then he fainted. A demonic battle for his soul was on.

Some deacons from the church found him in the bathroom, picked him up, and cleaned him up. They wanted to take him to his car, but he insisted on going back into the meeting. Almost as soon as he returned, he again began vomiting. Deacons once more tried to drag him out, but again he refused to go. At the end of my talk, Adrian was the first to come forward. Right there, at the altar of Iglesia Sobre la Roca, that young man was taken by God. "God changed him," Adrian said about me, "so I know he can change me too. I need the same love that changed him."

Several months later, a school official called the pastor of the church, Eric DiCesare, and asked him what had happened to Adrian. Adrian's life and attitude had changed so much that everyone around him noticed it and could hardly believe he was the same rebellious gangsta. Adrian gave away all his weapons and stopped hanging around with his former buddies in the gang. But he knew he wasn't ready to help others quite yet. He knew he had to grow in grace for a while before he could think about a ministry of his own. Adrian is smart.

The pastor and others took Adrian under their wing and began to teach him the way of God. They loved him like he had never been loved.

Upon giving his life to Christ, Adrian immediately resigned from the gangs. But when you join a gang, it is very difficult to leave once you have been initiated. Adrian immediately suffered persecution and received numerous death threats. One Sunday an enemy gang pulled up in a car outside the church, armed to the teeth with automatic weapons. They planned to kill Adrian right during the service. The pastor stopped preaching in the middle of his sermon, grabbed Adrian and snuck him out the back door.

Due to the harassment, Adrian moved to Chicago, but the threats followed him there. He returned to Houston, but was able

The Media Monster

We have a great responsibility to monitor what our children are being exposed to in the media. Television, movies, newspapers, and even video games these days are full of violence. Parents are shown killing children and vice versa.

Young people are being saturated with violence on TV, in movies, and in music. They are being brainwashed, and it's happening at such a young age—to children from eight to thirteen years old. I think the media is guilty of glorifying the bad and the ugly. And I'm not alone in my opinion.

Since the mid-1970s the gang problem has moved out of the home and into society. Modern television and media often feed the gang mentality, giving youth gangs the recognition they crave and the exposure they need to stay alive.... Movies like the recently released *Colors*... only glorify the gang mentality. *Colors*... has little base in fact, but has spread the gospel of gang life across many areas of the United States.

Since youth gangs became an issue in the United States... the media has served as a diffusion tool, bringing the gang message to youth in small towns across America. Far too often, the media also perpetuates the macho image that encourages violence.[S1]

Doug Allen, a detective on the gang task force in Toledo, Ohio, says media images such as the movie *Colors* have helped accelerate the gang problem in Toledo. Since that film, youths started acting and dressing like gang members. "I believe strongly that this is often a media-induced problem in the Midwest," Allen said. "The media have moved this problem ahead ten to twelve years in our area." *continued on facing page* to stay only for two months as the risk increased—not only to his life but to his mother's as well. In spite of all of this adversity, Adrian never turned his back on Jesus. Today he lives in Mexico and, according to him, he would rather die than go back to the gangs!

Sergeant Buz Williams of the Long Beach, California, Police Department told us that the news media often exacerbate an already bad situation. For instance, he cited a recent show featuring tagging, followed by a noticeable increase in graffiti. The gang members love their publicity!

Detective Jim Klisch of the Milwaukee gang crimes/intelligence unit agreed that the media play a role in the gang problem, and that they need to be more careful about how they present gang activities. He said people need to be informed, but that the media need to be careful not to glorify or exaggerate gang activities. For example, a police killing recently was claimed by the Conservative Vice Lords. After that report got out, many gang members started claiming to be members of the CVLs.

We need to encourage TV and radio stations to be more responsible. They could take a page out of the book at Los Angeles rap station KACE, which recently banned all songs that they thought glorified violence, gangs, drugs, overt sexuality, and denigration of women. The banned list includes "Indo Smoke," by Mista Grimm, which talks about the joys of marijuana use; "Freak Me," by Silk, which has sold one million copies and has a sexual reference about a man licking a woman; "Dre Day," by Dr. Dre, laden with guns and violence; "Downtown," by SWV, based on a double entendre that KACE music director Mark Gunn says is made clear in the group's video; "Insane in the Brain," by Cypress Hill, about pot; and "Lick U Up," by H-Town, which is sexually explicit.

Gunn said, "You have to look at the state of the black community. There are some very serious problems, from teenage pregnancies to drive-by shooting and very poor academic skills. With music being one of the main influences in some people's lives, you have to start somewhere."[52]

MY VISION OF THE FUTURE

It's young men like Alberto, Fernando, and Adrian who have turned my heart back to the gangs. Their stories have often caused me to break down in tears. This is where I belong. These are the people to whom God has called me to minister. I have been given the gift to communicate the gospel to these kids. Before Alberto, I had never said to a young man, "Come over here, son." It came out spontaneously. But that day it dawned on me, "Man, I'm a father. I'm a grandpa. I was once in this young man's shoes, and no one called me 'son.' I can help boys like this find the father they never had but desperately need."

What Can We Do about the Media?

It wouldn't hurt us to start paying more attention to voices that are thousands of years old. I'm thinking primarily of the Bible, but in this instance I'm also thinking about the ancient Greek philosopher, Plato. It was Plato who asked the citizens of his own day,

> Shall we just carelessly allow children to hear any casual tales which may be devised by casual persons, and to receive into their minds ideas for the most part the very opposite of those which we should wish them to have when they are grown up? We cannot.... Anything received into the mind at that age is likely to become indelible and unalterable; and therefore it is most important that the tales which the young first hear should be models of virtuous thoughts.[S1]

Gangs: The Epidemic Sweeping America advises that "parents should monitor their children's media exposure. The controversy over just how affected children are by music and television still rages on, but do you want to take that chance with your children?"[S2] Adds Colorado Springs Chief of Police Lorne Kramer, "Read what your child is listening to. If you take a look at the words, you might be shocked. Most parents would never allow language like that at the dinner table."[S3]

I have friends who have teenage kids. I have noticed that their
continued on facing page

That's when I knew I was being called back to the inner cities, to reach the gang members.

There is something definitely happening among the youth of this country. Gang leaders and gang members are coming forward in almost all of our services. There is a great unrest in the young people of this nation, and especially in those of the inner city. These people are growing tired of seeing their friends and brothers and sisters die from drug overdoses, from the bullets of an Uzi, from a disease contracted from a dirty needle. Remember seven-year-old Kenny Tillman of Mobile, Alabama, who told reporters he was "tired" of all the shootings in his neighborhood? People are becoming angry at seeing their sports heroes come tumbling to earth,

kids have changed. They are beginning to talk back to their parents, they have bad attitudes and seem not to care. In many of these instances, these kids spend a lot of time playing video games at home. I believe there is a strong correlation between the kids' bad behavior and the time they spend with the games.

These video games captivate the minds of the kids. The games are violent and gory, often with occultic undertones. The result is that the kids are no longer capable of distinguishing fantasy from reality. They become obsessed with the violence they see on the video screen, on TV, and at the movies. I remember that I was like this. I thought I was immortal. I never thought of the electric chair or death.

My real problem here is with the parents who have allowed these games and programs to invade their homes. Time that used to be spent together in family devotions or outings to the park now are replaced by the kids spending hours in front of a video screen. The parents try to pacify their kids, and they are not willing to stand up to them. We no longer have the courage or the "tough love" to raise our kids in a godly way.

I am against video games and anything else—TV, movies, magazines, whatever—that takes the place of our spending time with our children. We need to take a stand and fight for our homes. In this book we talk a lot about saving the youth of America. But as we concentrate on the gangs and the inner city, let's not lose the battle at home.

falling victim to venereal diseases and addictions. The children are crying for an answer, a hero, a savior.

I believe the next great revival and move of God will come not from big churches or ministries. It will not happen because of church or denominational board decisions. It will not happen by the will of man. Instead, it will come as an explosion from our inner cities and from the young people of this country who will stand up and cry: "No more dying! No more murders! No more diseases! No more evil!"

A Christian song from the early eighties by Randy Stonehill said that God is coming back for some angry young people: men and women who, in righteous anger, refuse to let their country go to hell. I truly believe that God will raise up millions of young intercessors who will take up the rallying cry of their nation and will invade the throne room of the Most High with their prayers, begging God for an answer, a release, a move of his Holy Spirit on this land.

My own office has been flooded with letters and phone calls both from this country and from around the world requesting—some almost begging—that we come and help them with their drug and gang problems. We are getting phone calls even from secular civic organizations. The communities of this nation are becoming desperate and are finding that mere social programs provide no lasting answers or solutions. That's why they are turning to Christian ministries almost as a last resort in an attempt to stop the tidal wave of violence.

More than one "expert" has written off the inner cities as war zones. They're not blind. They see that drug-related murder is on the rise. New York City alone reports one murder every five hours. That is nearly 1,800 homicides every year in one city alone. There are also 60,000 homeless in New York City, most of them living underground in the subway system in conditions unfit for an animal. At a point when our nation has the lowest unemployment rate in years, why are so many of our citizens suffering? When you witness whole families living in subways, sleeping under cardboard boxes, you have to ask: "O God, why? Why all of this suffering and misery?"

I believe that this satanic attack is directed not only at all of humanity but is primarily targeting the body of Christ. Since the devil cannot harm God, he is concentrating his efforts on destroying the next closest thing: God's children.

That is why I am so proud of the "square" kids. They are exposed to all the filth and the dirt that blight this generation, yet they stand tall and say, "I'm not going to get dirty. I'm not going to follow that lifestyle. I don't care if I'm going to be ridiculed. I'm not going to get dirty." My conversion was supernatural, but to be able to stay "square" is far more supernatural than that. These kids, both in the inner cities and in the suburbs, have decided to keep themselves square. This is a virtue that comes from the heart. I'm always going to take my hat off to these wonderful young people.

The square kids in the ghetto are the most powerful precisely because they refuse to get dirty. They stay clean despite the social pressure of loose morals. They are the overcomers. We must encourage them more—they have nothing to be ashamed of. Straight is beautiful!

The media, of course, doesn't report on the straight kids. But they are the real heroes. Recently on an airplane I met a guy who left his gang through the efforts of his girlfriend, a "straight" girl who never got dirty in the gangs. This guy and this girl grew up in the same neighborhood, faced the same kind of challenges and the same pressures, but she refused to get involved in what she knew to be wrong. This young man attributed his new life away from the gangs directly to her. She is a hero in my book!

THE BATTLE FOR OUR KIDS

We must pray as never before against the demonic influences that are threatening to destroy our nation and its people. We have to put on the armor of God daily and stand against the devil. We have to know the Bible, the sword of the Spirit, so that we can answer any doubt that Satan throws our way.

Probably the most powerful offensive weapon in our arsenal is prayer and intercession. As Ephesians 6 says: "Finally, be strong in the Lord and in his mighty power.... For our struggle is not against flesh and blood, but against the rulers, against the authorities, against the powers of this dark world and against the spiritual forces of evil in the heavenly realms." If we go into a difficult situation in prayer and know what we're doing, inside of five minutes we can make demons tremble. We don't have to be the ones who are intimidated!

We are the army of the Lord, his representatives and ambassadors to this world. We have an incredible responsibility, but we serve an incredible God who is able to do great things! Amazingly, he invites us to join him in his work.

Let's Be Adults about This

I was taking a flight home from Chicago many years ago, dead tired from a hectic week of crusade activities. The last thing I wanted to do was speak to somebody on the plane, so I took a window seat, crumpled into my little corner of the plane, fastened my seat belt, and closed my eyes as though I were going to sleep.

About thirty minutes into the flight, I looked up and noticed the gentleman sitting next to me. He seemed to be a very congenial fellow and saw me open my eyes. Since I didn't want to be rude, I said, "Hi." He said "Hi!" back to me, and so began a conversation I really didn't plan on having.

(I since have learned of a neat trick for cutting off airplane conversations that you don't want to have. Tony Campolo, an energetic college professor and author who also has a worldwide speaking ministry, says that he tailors the way he responds to questions about his vocation according to how much energy he has. If he boards a plane with a spring in his step, he'll tell the person sitting next to him that he works as a sociologist at a small college back East [Eastern College in Pennsylvania]. That always gets them curious and they want to know more. But if he's dead tired and doesn't want to talk to anybody, he'll identify himself as a Baptist evangelist. He says it works like magic—nobody wants to talk to him after that! Maybe I could do the same thing: If I want to talk, I'll tell them I'm a former gang member who works with at-risk youth. If I don't want to talk, I'll tell them I'm a *Pentecostal* evangelist! Maybe they'll get up and take a different seat!)

After we had talked for a few minutes, this gentleman looked at me and said, "I notice you have a heavy accent." Not "a sexy accent," which I really would have liked, but "a heavy accent."

"Yes," I said.

"What nationality are you?" he asked.

"I'm Puerto Rican," I told him. Immediately you could see the wheels spinning in the man's head as he started to put things together from our conversation.

"Oh," he said, "what's your name?"

"Nicky," I replied.

"Nicky Cruz?" he asked excitedly.

"Yes, sir."

"The same Nicky Cruz that's in *The Cross and the Switchblade* and *Run, Baby, Run?*" he asked. "You're *that* Nicky Cruz?"

"Yes, sir," I said. "That's me."

"I can't believe this!" he almost shouted. "Why, my wife adores you! She has prayed for you, my children have prayed for you—I mean, you have been in their hearts for a long time. They really love you! They've read all your books. And they love Jesus!"

No self-respecting evangelist could resist such an opening. "What about you?" I asked.

His enthusiasm dimmed noticeably, his head dropped a little, and he replied, "Well... no."

In a few moments the conversation began to turn around and I was the one who was asking the questions. "What do you do?" I asked. "What is your profession?"

To my complete surprise, the man told me he was an executive with a large tobacco company.

"Uh-huh—then what are you doing here in the no-smoking section?" I wondered aloud.

He laughed and said, "Well, I don't smoke. Smoking is bad for my health."

I'm serious—I'm telling you the truth! That's exactly what this executive of a huge cigarette company told me: "Smoking is bad for my health."

Hey, I'm Puerto Rican. How could I be quiet after that? I couldn't help blurting out, "Don't you feel guilty about the people who have cancer and the people who suffer and destroy themselves physically by using your product?"

"No, not at all" he replied calmly. "People have the warning labels right there on the cigarette cartons. The warnings tell them smoking is harmful, that it can lead to cancer. But you know something? People don't have any respect for the warnings. They have no regard for them at all. We have more people smoking now than we did ten years ago."

You could tell that he was proud of his achievement. He took on a challenge, and he was winning. He was just a successful businessman, that's all. His calloused attitude seemed to say, "Sure, I'm involved in creating and selling a product that kills people. In fact, I'm an executive with one of the largest companies around. And no, I wouldn't use the product myself—I don't want to die. But if people want to kill themselves, that's their choice. I'm not responsible. We tell them it's dangerous, don't we? I'm not the one who puts the cigarette in their mouths. Why should I be concerned about them? I'm comfortable. I make a good living. I take care of my own family. If others are stupid enough to kill themselves off by using my product, that's their problem. It's not my fault. I'm just a good businessman."

It's not a pretty argument, is it? You're probably as horrified by it as I was that day.

But you know something? That man isn't alone. I'm afraid the church suffers from exactly the same sort of attitude as that businessman.

WARNING LABELS AREN'T ENOUGH

Oh, the church isn't involved with manufacturing and selling cigarettes. It isn't trying to get people to smoke when it knows that smoking kills.

But it has turned its back on the suffering youth of this country who are dying at ever-younger ages and in ever-increasing numbers. We cluck our tongues at that businessman for trying to justify his job simply by citing the warning labels on cigarette cartons, but do we act much differently? The church is great at denouncing gang violence—our own "warning label"—but have we done anything about the problem? You see, it's not enough just to admit there's a problem. It's not enough to send out warnings.

It's time for action! But first, before we can move out effectively as a mighty army of the Lord, we have to admit our own guilt. We

---

Needed: Anchor Churches

Not surprisingly, researchers say dysfunctional families, substance abuse, television violence, child abuse, and poverty are to blame for the tragic state of today's youth culture. They also say that the declining influence of churches and schools has left children drifting without a moral anchor.

I'm glad to say that there are some churches that still provide a moral anchor. Many evangelicals are taking their Bibles seriously and are taking steps to raise the level of the whole neighborhood where they minister.

I think of Alejandro Montes, an Episcopalian pastor in Houston, Texas, who has taken up the challenge. He and his wife are full of Jesus and are committed evangelists. When young criminals started stealing his church's property and shooting out its windows, Alejandro and his wife began to get to work in their community. They overcame their intimidation, went to the youths, and invited them to come to their church. "This church is your church," Alejandro told them.

Gang members gradually started showing up both to worship and to use the facilities for recreation. Church members were taught to welcome the gang kids and to relate to them as if the members were the kids' big brothers.

The congregation's energetic spirit eventually became contagious and spread throughout the community. Crime has come down and the church is at the center of everything that's happening.

I just wish we had more churches and pastors with a similar vision! Without them, the violence will only increase and spread.

have to accept our part of the blame for allowing things to become as bad as they now are. We have to be adults about this and confess our own guilt in the slaughter of our youth.

I don't say this merely to make a dramatic point or to get a reaction. I say it because I know that until a large part of the church of Jesus Christ admits it has not fulfilled its mission in its own backyard, things will not change. If it's not really our fault, then why should we do anything about it? After all, isn't it enough to say how badly we feel about the mess "those people" are in? Isn't it enough to wish things were different?

In other words: If the warning labels are on the package, who can blame the manufacturer?

I think we all know the answer to that one.

CONFESSING OUR SINS LEADS TO HEALTH

Scripture doesn't instruct us to confess our sins because it likes being morbid. It doesn't command us to own up to our faults to make us feel guilty. It tells us to admit our wrongdoings because it knows that's the only way we can get back on the road to spiritual health:

> Therefore confess your sins to each other and pray for each other so that you may be healed. The prayer of a righteous man is powerful and effective. James 5:16

> When I kept silent, my bones wasted away through my groaning all day long. For day and night your hand was heavy upon me; my strength was sapped as in the heat of summer. Then I acknowledged my sin to you and did not cover up my iniquity. I said, "I will confess my transgressions to the LORD"—and you forgave the guilt of my sin. Psalm 32:3-5

When Daniel considered all the evil his people had done which led to their captivity in Babylon, he did not shrink from admitting his guilt as a fellow Israelite. "*We* have sinned and done wrong," he prayed. "*We* have been wicked and have rebelled; *we* have turned away from your commands and laws. *We* have not listened to your servants the prophets…. *We* are covered with shame…. All Israel has transgressed your law and turned away, refusing to obey you. Therefore the curses and sworn judgments written in the Law of Moses, the servant of God, have been poured out on *us*, because *we* have sinned against you. You have fulfilled the words spoken against *us* and against *our* rulers by bringing upon *us* great disaster" (Dn 9:5, 6, 10-12, emphasis added).

Don't forget that Daniel is one of only two major characters in the Old Testament about whom nothing negative is ever said. (Joseph is the other.) Yet this man, who walked close to God his entire, long life, was willing to admit his guilt as part of the guilt of his people. It wasn't *their* problem, it was *his* problem. And he knew to whom he was praying! Oh, did he know!

> Now, our God, hear the prayers and petitions of your servant. For your sake, O Lord, look with favor on your desolate sanctuary. Give ear, O God, and hear; open your eyes and see the desolation of the city that bears your Name. We do not make requests of you because we are righteous, but because of your great mercy. O Lord, listen! O Lord, forgive! O Lord, hear and act! For your sake, O my God, do not delay. **Daniel 9:17-19a**

Just as in Daniel's day, our land is dotted with "desolate" cities ravaged by sin, wickedness, and disobedience. Just as in Daniel's day, we do not ask God to intervene because we are so righteous or so holy or so good. No! Just as in Daniel's day, we make petitions for our cities and our youth because *he* is righteous, because *he* is holy, because *he* is good. We come boldly to the throne of grace because of *his* great mercy and because of what Jesus Christ accomplished on our behalf at the cross. That is why we can pray and expect God to listen, to forgive, to hear, and to act. And just as in Daniel's day, we must pray that there will be no delay in his answer.

But first—before any of this—we must admit that all of us, as members of the church of Jesus Christ, have failed to do what we have been called to do. We have not obeyed the Great Commission, which tells us to "go and make disciples of all nations"—including those in the ghettos, including those in the barrios, including those in South Central Los Angeles and the South Side of Chicago and the mean streets that span this country—"baptizing them in the name of the Father and of the Son and of the Holy Spirit, and teaching them to obey everything that I have commanded you" (Mt 28:19, 20a).

We must openly and in repentance admit that we have abdicated our responsibility to act as adults, and that our kids are dying as a result. We must confess that we have not been the role models we need to be, and that our kids have become lost and confused because of it.

JUDGMENT IN THE HOUSE OF GOD

It is time that we take seriously what God says to us in all of Scripture, especially in a passage such as 1 Peter 4:17-18:

> For it is time for judgment to begin with the family of God; and if it begins with us, what will the outcome be for those who do not obey the gospel of God? And, "If it is hard for the righteous to be saved, what will become of the ungodly and the sinner?"

We ignore God's instructions at our own risk. Through the apostle Paul, the Lord told us that we are in a spiritual war. We are not visiting an amusement park or strolling through a lovely garden, but are stationed on a bloody field of battle.

It is time to admit that we have forgotten all this. The reason the church has lost its power is that it has lost its memory of who and what it is. Somehow we have failed to remember that the body of Christ is "a chosen people, a royal priesthood, a holy nation, a people belonging to God." And we as its members have forgotten that we were given a specific task: "that you may declare the praises of him who called you out of darkness into his wonderful light" (1 Pt 2:9).

Happily, not all of us have forgotten these things. In November

1994, America's Roman Catholic bishops, alarmed that the country was becoming numb to the violence that increasingly infects all aspects of our nation's life, issued a sweeping denunciation of the "culture of violence" that now plagues American society. Their message was aimed not only at euthanasia, abortion, and the death penalty, but also at violence on television and in movies—and even in the frustrations that people act out when they're behind the wheel. The bishops said the root of the problem is a "violence of the heart," in which self-concern becomes more important than the common good.

Gun-Toting Children

I believe we can get a clear hint about our disturbing future simply by looking at what's happening in other nations where violence has become a way of life (or more likely, death). Consider Mozambique, a former Portuguese colony in Africa, as one such example.

The International Committee on Crisis Control has ranked Mozambique as the country with the greatest toll of human suffering in the world. War has been a way of life there for more than two decades. Children have suffered enormously, and many have been forced to serve in one or another faction as soldiers. The two most powerful factions are the Renamo (the Mozambican National Resistance movement, called bandits by most in the country; it has control of large portions of territory and is known for terrorist violence) and the Frelimo. Consider the story of Fernando:

By the time he was thirteen, Fernando had murdered six people. When the bandits overran his village, killing his parents, they found a well-muscled adolescent who could carry heavy loads long distances and, with training, become an efficient killer. First, Fernando was taught to kill birds and animals. He was beaten and deprived of food. Then he was given the blood of an ostrich. Drink it, Fernando was told; it will make you strong. By the time he was fourteen, Fernando Maposse was leading a group of more than a

continued on facing page

"Culturally, we are condoning and putting up with far too much in our media, our general approach to living and the way we relate to one another," said Bishop John Ricard, an auxiliary bishop in Baltimore and chairman of the Domestic Policy Committee of the National Conference of Catholic Bishops. "We've gotten so far afield from a clear sense of what is right and wrong, that there are principles and values that are transcendent and that are absolutely right and wrong."[1]

Other voices agree. *Sojourners* editor Jim Wallis said, "The cruel and endemic economic injustice, soul-killing materialism, life-

---

dozen other Renamo soldiers, all younger than he. Fernando is pretty sure he killed six people, he says, because he saw them die. But there may have been more.[51]

Experts say Fernando's prospects for a full life are "bleak" at best. "Children everywhere learn that it is wrong to kill and to hurt, and Fernando feels rage, and sometimes embarrassment, at what he was made to do," said the article which told Fernando's agonizing story, "and yet it cannot be undone. So for that reason, it is likely that Fernando, and the thousands of children like him, may never be able to reassemble the wreckage of their lives."[52]

I am so sorry that this comment is painfully true. But it is not inevitable! I can look back at my own years as a little boy who grew numb because of what happened in my childhood. I came from a "super-extra-dysfunctional family" and witnessed some of the most horrible incidents that any child could see. Yet God saved me from all of that and put me into the ministry of the gospel.

I have seen hundreds of children in the inner cities who are growing up in despicable circumstances, but who somehow are resisting the evil and are seeking hope and something good and lasting. I place a lot of emphasis in my crusades on children to come forward to receive Jesus. Fernando's story shows us how hard core some children can become; but I have seen countless kids who have suffered similar things, yet who still care about people.

destroying drug traffic, pervasive racism, unprecedented breakdown of family life and structure, and almost total collapse of moral values that have created this culture of violence are, at heart, spiritual issues."[2]

I agree with Wallis: Spiritual issues are at the heart of our problems. The church has compromised in the two critical areas of holiness and evangelism, and therefore has lost its power as an agent of change. So we are back to the fable of the cat and the bird that I told in the introduction to this book. Our feathers are almost gone, and the cat is about to pounce. If we are to make a difference in our decaying society, we must admit that this is our true predicament. We must get to the spiritual roots of the problem: We must correct our faulty views of what holiness really is; and we must recommit ourselves to evangelism. Without addressing these two key issues, I see no hope for America. But if we *do* get serious about both of them, the hope is literally out of this world!

REGAINING THE FEAR OF THE LORD

"Violence in American society reflects a lack of the fear of God," wrote Caleb Rosado in *Christianity Today*.

The carnage in our cities raises a crucial question: Where is God? Or, more precisely, where is the sense of the holiness and awesomeness of God to whom one must give account? The Bible calls this sense the "fear of God." It does not mean fear in our usual sense of being afraid. It means rather to quake or tremble in the presence of a Being so holy, so morally superior, so removed from evil, that in his presence, human boasting, human pride, human arrogance vanish as we bow in speechless humility, reverence, and adoration of the One beyond understanding.

For this reason, Proverbs declares, "The fear of the Lord is the beginning of wisdom." Any correct understanding of the human condition begins with a sense of the presence of God in human affairs. When the fear of God is missing, evil, corruption, and violence prevail. "Fools say in their hearts, 'There is no God.' They are corrupt, they do abominable deeds; there is no one who does good" (Ps 14:1).... The psalmist says, "Transgression speaks to the wicked deep in their hearts!" (Ps 36:1, RSV). Why? "There is no fear of God before their eyes." Abraham went down to Egypt and feared for his life. He declared, 'I thought, "There is no fear of God at all in this place, and they will kill me"' (Gn 20:11, RSV).

Where God is not feared, life is cheap.[3]

I think Rosado is exactly right. The church has wandered from a biblical idea of holiness and has put in its place a man-made code of regulations that have little to do with the fear of the Lord. If we are to make a difference in this society, we must recover the kind of firm but gentle holiness that comes from a genuine fear of God. "We must restore to our communities a sense of awe toward God," Rosado writes. "A renewed sense of God's awesomeness will supply the security and purpose our culture is seeking. Only by being assured of God's love for us do we learn to love ourselves. And only by being assured of God's love for all people do we learn to imitate his example (Mt 5:44-48)."[4]

The world has had its fill of harsh, judgmental Christians who know nothing of the meekness of holiness. If we are to change our world, we must start with ourselves. We must rediscover the fear of God and allow it to build into our lives the most beautiful, gentle, meek spirit of holiness. Then the message we speak with our mouths will find receptive ears anxious to hear about the holy God who loves us so much he sacrificed the life of his only Son.

THE PRIORITY OF EVANGELISM

Because we have not been people who fear God, we have allowed evangelism to take a backseat in all our activities. We are simply not trying to reach people with the saving gospel of Jesus Christ. That is the bottom-line reason why we are in such a mess.

As an evangelist since 1966, I have been to many cities, towns, and communities. I have noticed that in the past twenty years music festivals, teaching seminars, and prophetic conferences (to name a few) have taken the place of evangelism. The focus is not on others, but on ourselves. "How can my life have more meaning to me?" we are asking ourselves.

And yet America in the nineties has become one of the most desperate mission fields in the world. Our own backyard is in great neglect. My heart breaks as I sense this rejection of evangelism, which is the message God has given me. I understand the prophet Jeremiah who wept because of the condition of his people. Jesus' first love is reaching out to hurting people—in other words, evangelism.

In Revelation 2:4-5, the Holy Spirit calls out to the church at Ephesus (and to us), "Yet I hold this against you: you have forsaken your *first* love [emphasis added]." The first love of the early church was the message of repentance from sin, brought about by the resurrection of Jesus Christ from the dead. Jesus conquered both sin and death in order to give us a changed life.

The Ephesian church had discernment and perseverance, but stayed locked within its four walls where its members felt safe. Yet the Holy Spirit pleads with them to "remember the height from which you have fallen. Repent and do the things you did at first." That is, get back to evangelism!

I can remember only two times in the entire Bible where God is said to be "sick." The first is in Genesis, during Noah's day when the Lord had to destroy the earth in a worldwide flood. The second is found in Revelation (3:16), when Jesus threatened to vomit the Ephesian church out of his mouth.

I am convinced that the biggest sin of the church today is an overwhelming lack of evangelism. This lack, as I have said, is tied to our failure to fear God. Listen to the apostle Paul once more:

Since, then, we know what it is to fear the Lord, we try to persuade men.... For Christ's love compels us.... All this is from God, who reconciled us to himself through Christ and gave us the ministry of reconciliation: that God was reconciling the world to himself in Christ, not counting men's sins against them.

And he has committed to us the message of reconciliation. We are therefore Christ's ambassadors, as though God were making his appeal through us. We implore you on Christ's behalf: Be reconciled to God. God made him who had no sin to be sin for us, so that in him we might become the righteousness of God.

2 Corinthians 5:11, 14, 18-21

Every person who names the name of Christ must be involved in evangelism. We need every Christian to be active in sharing the Good News. If we don't get back into the mainstream of evangelism, we won't be able to save this country. If we don't address the spiritual roots of our problem, there's no way we can succeed.

I think we are afraid to be rejected, ridiculed, pushed, or slapped for the sake of the Lord Jesus. We need to be encouraged more often by the message of 1 Peter 4:13-16:

But rejoice that you participate in the sufferings of Christ, so that you may be overjoyed when his glory is revealed. If you are insulted because of the name of Christ, you are blessed, for the Spirit of glory and of God rests on you…. If you suffer as a Christian, do not be ashamed, but praise God that you bear that name.

What is the key to such bold witness? It's found just a little earlier in 1 Peter, where the apostle instructs us, "'Do not fear what they fear; do not be frightened.' But in your hearts set apart Christ as Lord. Always be prepared to give an answer to everyone who asks you to give the reason for the hope that you have. But do this with gentleness and respect, keeping a clear conscience, so that those who speak maliciously against your good behavior in Christ may be ashamed of their slander. It is better, if it is God's will, to suffer for doing good than for doing evil" (1 Pt 3:14b-17).

The key is to keep Jesus at the forefront of your consciousness. We would not be afraid of the devil and his slimy tactics if our minds were full of the glory of God!

BUT I DON'T HAVE THE GIFT!

The witness to which all Christians are called is not to be confused with the spiritual gift of evangelism. All believers are to witness.

Not all are given the gift of evangelism, but witnessing must not be written off for that reason as somebody else's responsibility. Too often believers think, *If only I can get somebody to come to my church, then the pastor's words will convert them.* Well, believe it or not, the testimony of a concerned friend can be far more effective than a sermon from a stranger in a pulpit.

Outsiders are first drawn to Christians and then to Christ. Many times, a sermon may convict a sinner—but it is the loving concern of a Christian that brings them to a personal relationship with Jesus!

You can win people who will not listen to a preacher. You're not a distant clergyman in a suit. You are just you—a friend who cares. The Lord has placed you in the nonbeliever's life for a reason and has given you the opportunity and responsibility to be his witness.

What a tragedy, my friend, if on the Day of Judgment you are about to be welcomed to your heavenly reward and as you step forward, a condemned friend cries out in agony, "Why didn't you tell me how to live forever? Why didn't you say something?"

At some point, all of us are called to present the words of the salvation message. If we know enough to be saved ourselves, we know enough to relate the basic gospel.

I didn't go to Bible school before I began proclaiming the Good News to my fellow gang members. The Holy Spirit was my teacher—and will be yours. Remember that you can't bring anybody to the point of accepting salvation. It is the Holy Spirit who quickens God's words, brings conviction of sin, and causes the nonbeliever to accept salvation. The Holy Spirit will give you power. We can depend on him to provide us with the necessary words.

Let's cut to the chase: Do you know someone who needs the Savior?

Then pray for them. Pray for their needs. Pray that you will care about them in a new and powerful way. Pray for the ministering of the Holy Spirit as you go out with the gospel in the name of Jesus.

And consider these words from the apostle Paul in 1 Thessalonians 1:5-6 (KJV): "For our gospel came not unto you in word only, but also in power, and in the Holy Ghost, and in much assurance; as ye know what manner of men we were among you for your sake. And ye became followers of us, and of the Lord, having received the word in much affliction, with joy of the Holy Ghost."

We need to regain the heart for evangelism that we've lost. We need to be praying that the Holy Spirit will break down walls, make the church transparent, take the message of Christ to the streets. That's the *only* way we will see victory in this battle.

Caleb Rosado ended the article that I quoted earlier with a very moving story. "Driving home from San Francisco recently," he wrote, "I pulled off Highway 101 to pay tribute at the informal memorial set up there in remembrance of Polly Klaas, the twelve-year-old girl who was kidnapped... during a slumber party and later killed. It was a sobering experience, recalling her death at the hands of a heartless killer. Of all the kind words expressed there on cards, paper scraps, and wood, one moved me to the core. It simply read, 'For a brief moment an angel rested here.'

"If Polly's life had been respected, if her abductor had seen the sacred in her, she would still be with us. We too must learn to glimpse that unique image of God that dwells in every person. As we do, we can begin the process of rebuilding a society where differences can be valued and where children like Polly will be safe."[5]

Remember, our war is not fought with grenades and machine guns and missiles. We do not fight with bayonets and flame throwers and howitzers. We need ministries geared to mix fire with fire: They shoot bullets, we're going to shoot Scriptures. They threaten, we bless. They dispense hate, we give love. "We work hard with our own hands. When we are cursed, we bless; when we are persecuted, we endure it; when we are slandered, we answer kindly" (1 Cor 4:12-13).

We must remember too that the front lines in this war are not self-supporting. They need ammunition and supplies. They are chronically short-supplied, yet they slowly gain ground. They do not have the time to organize fund-raising campaigns or the expertise to motivate the larger churches to give. Many ministries can concentrate their efforts on producing a new "tape of the month" to bring in monthly revenue, but these frontline troops don't have that luxury.

I don't mean to be critical of the body of Christ for being fed through these inspirational tapes and teachings, but I do want to emphasize that our inner-city workers are not constantly receiving a new revelation from the Lord: they are simply trying to carry out the two-thousand-year-old mandate, "Go ye into all the world and make disciples." Their primary mission is evangelism, and it is clear and direct and ordained by God, with the power to break the chains of sin and bondage and set the captives free.

Evangelism is "to instruct in the gospel, to preach the gospel, and to convert." I am living proof of evangelism's power and effectiveness. Before someone told me about Christ, it was as if I were drowning in the ocean, fighting vicious undercurrents that were pulling me down. When someone at last told me that God loved me and sent his Son Jesus to die so that my sins could be forgiven and that I might live an abundant life, it was as if a life preserver had suddenly been thrown to me, which I clung to and held on to for dear life.

Many people think that television is going to change the world for God. No! What is going to change the world is every individual telling another individual, heart to heart, that they can make it. With this simple, "primitive" process, more people can be changed than if all our airwaves were filled with preachers and sermons. People need a human touch. They need to see someone who is making it.

That's the only way to win this war. Evangelism is our "secret weapon." But let's not make it so secret that nobody knows about it!

WHERE DO WE GO FROM HERE?

The issue is clear. It's black and white, with no gray areas. I've given it to you as straight as I can. We're in a big mess, and we're the reason for a lot of it. That's the nitty-gritty truth. We, the church of Jesus Christ, have abdicated our God-given roles to be salt and light. We have forgotten what true holiness is and have therefore ceased to make evangelism a priority.

The truth is not pretty, but it's truth all the same. Now it's up to us, as adults, to admit our mistakes, confess our sins, and move on into obedience.

We can't abandon the inner city; we must be a tower of strength *in* the city. We must rise to meet this new challenge with new ideas, new partnerships, new resolve. We must commit to work with people of like mind, and then cut them loose to see what God might be pleased to do through them.

The Catholic bishops I mentioned earlier called for individuals and parishes to investigate how they might best respond to the violence in their neighborhoods. They suggested possible actions that could be taken in both the church's liturgy and in social action, ideas ranging from appropriate readings and blessings to clothing drives, shelters for battered women, and organized anti-violence campaigns. They also cited a number of successful local efforts, including the Pittsburgh Diocese, part of a coalition that includes the city government and businesses which are interested in developing employment and educational programs for at-risk youth.

A GIANT ASLEEP

The church of the Lord is a sleeping giant. That is both my greatest regret and my greatest hope. The money of America still says, "In God We Trust." We still hear echoes of the Puritans, who rose from second-class citizenship in England to lead the spiritual and economic development of the New World.

I believe with all my heart that soon America will become sick and tired of licking its wounds. It will grow weary of hurting—and the church of the Lord will be ready to take its rightful place as a Holy Ghost Hospital, fully staffed by people who fear the Lord, who serve in the meekness of holiness, and who are committed with all their hearts to evangelism.

We need vision, we need courage. Scores of churches all across this nation have caught the vision and are encouraging others to join them. As I said, we'll be looking at them. But we won't look to admire them only. We'll look at what they're doing to encourage us, to use them as a model for our own efforts.

And we really must make those efforts! That is both our great privilege and our great responsibility. In the midst of an age that forgets, let us not forget the sobering words of James:

> What good is it, my brothers, if a man claims to have faith but has no deeds? Can such faith save him? Suppose a brother or sister is without clothes and daily food. If one of you says to him, "Go, I wish you well; keep warm and well fed," but does nothing about his physical needs, what good is it? In the same way, faith by itself, if it is not accompanied by action, is dead.
>
> James 2:14-17

They're Stealing the Souls of Our Children

Little seven-year-old Kenny Tillman was playing outside his apartment at the Happy Hills community in north Mobile, Alabama, at about 5 P.M. on October 24, 1994. It was just an ordinary day until a man wearing a white T-shirt and black pants took out a pistol and shot to death forty-year-old Theodis Ridgeway, or "Buddy Man" as he was known on the streets.

Kenny witnessed the whole scene. He saw the gun, he saw the flash, he saw Buddy Man fall, he saw the blood. Tragically, it wasn't the first time his little eyes had been exposed to events similarly lethal. Kenny's mother, Boddy Tillman, said her son is afraid to sleep alone because of the frequent shootings in Happy Hills. Kenny himself summed up his little-boy feelings about the violence by saying he was "tired of it." "It's scary," said his mother, "we don't know what we will do, just try to stay in the house, just avoid everything."[1]

But even more, let us not forget the prophecy of our Lord himself. As he neared the end of his own earthly ministry, he took time out to weave a startling picture of future days that should be joyfully anticipated by some, but feared and dreaded by others. Here is what he said:

> When the Son of Man comes in his glory, and all the angels with him, he will sit on his throne in heavenly glory. All the nations will be gathered before him, and he will separate the people one from another as a shepherd separates the sheep from the goats. He will put the sheep on his right and the goats on his left.
>
> Then the King will say to those on his right, "Come, you who are blessed by my Father; take your inheritance, the kingdom prepared for you since the creation of the world. For I was hungry and you gave me something to eat, I was thirsty and you gave me something to drink, I was a stranger and you invited me in, I needed clothes and you clothed me, I was sick and you looked after me, I was in prison and you came to visit me."
>
> Then the righteous will answer him, "Lord, when did we see you hungry and feed you, or thirsty and give you something to drink? When did we see you a stranger and invite you in, or needing clothes and clothe you? When did we see you sick or in prison and go to visit you?"
>
> The King will reply, "I tell you the truth, whatever you did for one of the least of these brothers of mine, you did for me."
>
> Then he will say to those on his left, "Depart from me, you who are cursed, into the eternal fire prepared for the devil and his angels. For I was hungry and you gave me nothing to eat, I was thirsty and you gave me nothing to drink, I was a stranger and you did not invite me in, I needed clothes and you did not clothe me, I was sick and in prison and you did not look after me."
>
> They also will answer, "Lord, when did we see you hungry or thirsty or a stranger or needing clothes or sick or in prison, and did not help you?"

He will reply, "I tell you the truth, whatever you did not do for one of the least of these, you did not do for me."

Then they will go away to eternal punishment, but the righteous to eternal life.   Matthew 25:31-46

I choose to believe that you and I will be in the blessed group, not the second! I choose to believe that we will buckle the belt of truth about our waists, put the breastplate of righteousness in its proper place, and get our feet fitted with the preparation of the gospel of peace. And by taking up the helmet of salvation and the sword of the Spirit, the Word of God, we will move out together as a mighty army under the direction of our head, the Lord Jesus Christ.

That will be a sight to see! That will be a joy to behold! That will be a holy army to send the demons of hell running for cover!

And that is the soon-coming day for which I and many others are praying with all our hearts. I wonder—what does your heart tell you?

CHAPTER 6

The Victory of Reaching Out

On a beautiful, sunny Sunday morning not too long ago, I visited a congregation packed in for the second of three Sunday worship services at Victory Outreach of La Puente, California.[1] The church meets in the auditorium of what was once an abandoned East Los Angeles public high school, just a few miles from where the 1992 L.A. riots erupted. A real estate salesman might diplomatically tell you the church is located in a "transitional" neighborhood. Nearby homes appear to be low-income, many of them rental—cinder-block, flat-top 1960s housing development homes, some with stripped cars on sparse lawns and peeling paint on the eaves. But to the people of Victory Outreach, it is home.

The La Puente congregation stands, singing fervent praises with a spontaneity worthy of the best evangelical congregations. The people clap along as the worship leader begins a familiar chorus, their joy deep and from the heart. They are glad to be here. So am I.

The fifteen-hundred-seat sanctuary serves a church of thirty-five hundred members and looks like hundreds of others across America—slightly worn carpeting, hundreds of matching, padded metal chairs and large loudspeakers hanging from a low ceiling. The enthusiastic people are dressed in their Sunday best. As they come in, many are carrying large Bibles and Sunday school handouts.

Together, we begin a traditional hymn sung with infectious devotion. There are shouts of joy. The crowd is obviously young—predominantly parents with grade-schoolers and junior high youngsters.

Still, there is a sprinkling of gray throughout the crowd—grandparents with and without families. Singles dot the congregation too, and up front, filling several rows, are quite a few men ranging in age from their mid-twenties to early sixties. They are residents of a couple of nearby "rehabs"—Victory Outreach-sponsored rehabilitation homes. Each is fighting his own personal battle with alcohol, drugs, or even an addiction to street violence. As they wait for the service to begin, all carry Bibles. Just before the service, several were studiously flipping through the Word, jotting notes into spiral-bound journals.

Some of the rough-looking men seated around the building served as nonviolent warriors who—armed with only their faith—stood faithful in the midst of the 1992 riot, even as an angry mob advanced with guns and fire bombs. They are veterans of the human chain that prayerfully surrounded the South Central mission church's building while the rest of the neighborhood burned.

Welcome to the original Victory Outreach "addicts' church" (a label, by the way, the church itself no longer uses).

As I look around at the happy people filling row after row, I can easily see why a visitor might wonder how such a vibrant congregation could get such a strange nickname. There are no addicts writhing on the floor in narcotics withdrawal. No pushers are peddling their death to the crowd. No one slinks around here, ashamed of a shady past. Heads are held high—humbly dignified. There is no self-centered snobbishness nor self-conscious defensiveness.

Because I am not a casual visitor here, I know the history of this great congregation. Even today, most new members come from jails, poor neighborhoods, nonreligious families, drug treatment centers, the streets, and crack houses. It is not uncommon to see the crude tattoos of gang affiliation plastered up and down the arms of the faithful. These people singing so beautifully and enthusiastically come here from the mean sidewalks of this lower-income neighborhood and the barrios and government housing projects that surround it.

The ushers, some in their forties and fifties or even older, are all large men. All wear fashionable ties and sport sharp haircuts. But even on their hands and necks you spot rough, faded, homemade tattoos, the sort that one sees in prison and among street gang kids. Some of the tattoos have been obliterated, much like graffiti on a gas station's bathroom wall—filled in, drawn over so that one can only guess at what the original raunchy message might have been.

Many of these attentive, friendly ushers have tiny earpieces—like Secret Service agents who secure areas about to be visited by the President of the United States. At the belts of many of them are small walkie-talkies into which they occasionally speak.

"Some people are offended by our security team," admits one older usher with an earplug wire dangling to his lapel. He shrugs. "I just praise God that I can serve as I am needed."

My longtime friend, Sonny Arguinzoni, is the pastor of this remarkable church. I first knew this middle-aged servant of God as a teenage heroin junkie. He was a desperate heroin addict who had been through hospital-administered treatments no less than ten times in such places as the Lexington, Kentucky, Federal Hospital for Substance Abuse. He was in and out of jail countless times. Eventually I basically had to threaten him into giving up his habit. (This was right after I came to the Lord; my methods have changed considerably since that time!)

I was the director of the first Teen Challenge in Brooklyn, New York, when a skinny, strung-out heroin addict came stumbling in through the front door. This special memory is as fresh in my mind as if it had happened yesterday.

I had used drugs in the gangs, but I was never addicted or dependent on them. I wasn't hooked. Then here comes Sonny, a known addict, frequent patient at hospitals, and petty thief. During that time, in the early sixties, New York City had perhaps 100,000 drug addicts. Heroin was taking over. This was the beginning of the nightmare for the USA, a time that would eventually usher in the production and consumption of designer drugs, some more deadly and powerful than heroin and LSD. Then Sonny, a hardened, hopeless addict, had a beautiful conversion.

That was back when Sonny and I were both street kids. Soon after I came to faith, Sonny became my own "Timothy," my son in the faith, the first person I ever discipled. Now I count him as perhaps my closest friend and his church as one of my favorite congregations in the world.

It's not just "family ties" that bond my heart to Sonny and his church, however. It's the ministry that Victory Outreach is so effectively doing. Fuller Theological Seminary recently cited Victory Outreach as an example of a church that does a superb job of putting its people into ministry and directing their efforts in an effective, "hands-off" way.

One big difference between this church and many others today: The church does not encourage "transfer members." No effort is made to recruit Christians from other Los Angeles churches to fill the services at Victory Outreach. Most of the adults here are first-generation believers, redeemed off the hard streets of East Los Angeles. A large percentage graduate into leadership roles, and hundreds of Victory Outreach converts have been sent out to start new churches. Many of them are former drug addicts, like Sonny.

The church's formal mission statement says, "Victory Outreach is an international, church-oriented Christian ministry called to the task of evangelizing and discipling the hurting people of the world with the message, hope, and plan of Jesus Christ. This call involves a commitment to plant and develop churches, rehabilitation homes, and training centers in strategic cities of the world. Victory Outreach inspires and instills within people the desire to fulfill their potential in life with a sense of dignity, belonging, and destiny. Victory Outreach works cooperatively with others of mutual purpose in accomplishing the task before us."

It's a mission statement I positively adore.

IN THE BEGINNING

In the mid-sixties, at separate times, Sonny and I both attended a Bible school just down the street from the La Puente church. After Sonny finished his courses, he joined me in evangelistic work. But soon God put a restlessness in his heart, and Sonny began to see a need for a church where former addicts and felons could bring their families to worship God, unashamed of their pasts. He was convinced of their need for a church where they could grow and mature as Christians and fully participate in the life of a Christ-centered congregation.

So he went to work.

Sonny and his new bride, Julie, began by going into the rough Maravilla neighborhood of East Los Angeles. He spent his days and nights on the streets, talking to junkies and gang members who were wasting their lives on drugs and the violence of gang honor.

Sonny began taking men into his own home to help them kick their drug habits. There, Julie fed them and helped minister to them. She had grown up in Los Angeles and attended Bible school with the intention of becoming a missionary, but she willingly found a new ministry in the heart of the city. Sonny continued to bring hurting people home, and before long one after another gave their lives to Jesus. At one time, Sonny and Julie had fifty recovering addicts living in their small home. Yet neither considered it a hardship to try to raise a family of five while helping desperate addicts straighten out their lives.

"It was very good for my children," Julie says. "Every day, they saw God working miraculously in our lives. They saw hearts soften. They saw food that God put on the table when there was no money to feed fifty people. They saw Jesus heal in a mighty way."

But first Sonny had to prove himself. When he first came to California, the addicts and junkies didn't believe his story. He was a Puerto Rican like me from the East Coast. He completely changed cultures and went to the predominantly Mexican area of East Los Angeles. He began witnessing for Jesus and evangelizing—without help from anyone. He just felt strongly in his heart about going. When he infiltrated the neighborhoods and territories of the drug addicts, he understood it very well. Drug addicts are the same regardless of nationality or location. He began to meet addicts and tell them about Jesus and what he had done for him. He would say, "I was a junkie, but now I'm clean, I'm free. I have been to all kinds of hospitals and everyone had given up on me. The psychiatrists, the psychologists. Then Jesus Christ set me free!"

Sonny was young and naive. Maybe he thought the addicts would welcome him with open arms and beg him to pray for them.

Instead he found them to be skeptical and cynical. They taunted and challenged Sonny: "Man, you're full of bull! You're lying. Who do you think you are, coming over here and trying to act like you're one of us, like you understand our problems and our hangups? If you were an addict, show us! Show us the difference!"

In that moment Sonny reacted spontaneously. He rolled up his shirt sleeve, and there was the proof: the marks of a drug addict. There were his veins that had collapsed. He said, "This is my evidence! This is when I was a drug addict. This is when I was a slave. This was my lady, my destiny, my mistress, my wife, my girlfriend, my food, my everything, my reason, my passion. This is what dominated me. Death! And then Jesus came into my life with a message. There was Nicky Cruz, who was there beside me as a soldier, as a brother when I was wounded and an outcast. When all other people gave up on me, Jesus came into my life. Yes, the temptation was there. Yes, I wanted to quit and run away. Yes, I was sick. Yes, I was vomiting. But there was somebody who spent time beside my bed as I went through withdrawal, cold turkey, reading the Bible to me and praying with me. He was there putting a cold towel on my forehead as my body was going through convulsions. And it worked! It was a mixture of divine love and human love that did it."

It was then, after Sonny's conversion, that the breakthrough with Teen Challenge came. Sonny was the pioneer of the miracles that God had begun. Show me the difference? I will show you the difference—thousands and thousands of drug addicts who have been miraculously reached. Their lives are changed because we have shown the difference. We have shown our "tracks." We are ready to show the difference, to show that God has completely changed millions of people—rich and poor, from the ghetto to the suburbs. This is what the world is looking for: proof. And that is what the church has to be willing to show them.

Sonny will die with the evidence of his "tracks." They prove that he is an ex-junkie saved by the grace of God. That was the beginning of revival.

In 1967 the Arguinzonis purchased an old building on Gless Street and pursued Sonny's personal vision of reaching out to street people, winning them to Jesus, teaching them, raising them into leadership and evangelism, then sending them out to drug-infested neighborhoods. They began targeting tough neighborhoods such as Pico Rivera, Compton, North Soto Street, and even notorious East Florence Street, where the riots of 1992 exploded.

A WORLDWIDE MINISTRY EXPANDS

Today there are more than 150 Victory Outreach sites, each of them loosely affiliated with one of America's largest denominations. There are forty-one Victory Outreach congregations in California (at last count) in such cities as Antelope Valley, Bakersfield, Escondido, Fresno, and others. Some congregations have taken root in such notorious neighborhoods as South Central L.A., ground zero of the Rodney King riots.

Other Victory Outreaches are found in the roughest neighborhoods of cities such as Phoenix, Denver, Chicago, Baltimore, Detroit, Las Vegas, Newark, New York City, and Washington, D.C. There are eight Victory Outreaches in Mexico, three in the worst sections of urban Holland, as well as in the meanest districts of Barcelona, Spain; Santiago, Chile; London, England; São Paulo, Brazil; Dublin, Ireland; and the Republic of Togo's capital city of Tome.

Most of these churches have two or three rehabs which welcome new converts. These men and women usually need somewhere to live while they kick drug or alcohol addictions or overcome compulsive habits such as gambling, sexual excess, or thrill violence.

The rehabs are an integral part of Victory Outreach's worldwide ministry. "You know, Nicky," Sonny told me, "you and I learned in the early years in Brooklyn that you can't merely tell somebody on the street the gospel, lead them in the sinner's prayer, and, if they accept Jesus, just tell them to go in peace. No. We have to help them straighten up their lives if they want our help. And they usually do."

The work isn't easy—not by a long shot. Let me give you just one example.

On a Friday evening Sonny was giving me a tour of the La Puente facilities, especially the church nursery—so he could show off his newest grandchild—when he happened to poke his head into a junior high classroom where ten church volunteers were conducting discussion groups with a dozen street kids.

Several of the thirteen- and fourteen-year olds in the room were acting bored with religious talk and were scrawling gang graffiti on the classroom chalkboard, using colored chalk from the teacher's desk.

"Watch yourself," Sonny warned softly. "Some of these little guys are stone killers"—cold-blooded murderers. Life and death don't mean much to many of these kids. Some have watched as their own parents were shot to death. And many of their friends have ended up in graves long before their time.

In fact, during one recent month, five kids of this age from Victory Outreach were killed in gang warfare. Sonny officiated at all their funerals. There is a steely coldness in the eyes of several of these junior-high-age boys, a deadness. Even in the most baby-faced, there is a studied seriousness that is unnerving.

I asked one of the kids what it was like to grow up in East L.A. "Here in Bassett, your piece is your best friend," volunteered a thir-teen-year-old. A piece is a gun. Did he pack a "piece"? He looked up and stared at me, then warily admitted only that a "homie" of his brother carried a nine-millimeter pistol to school. Why does he carry a gun? The boy shrugged and spouted off a popular saying: "Rather be judged by twelve than carried by six"—meaning it is better to be judged by twelve jurors in court for carrying a gun than to be carried away in a casket by six pallbearers.

Such are the men and women, boys and girls to whom Victory Outreach ministers. As I said, it's not an easy ministry, nor is it free from danger.

Just after sunset one day in Pomona, California, perhaps one hundred neighborhood kids and teens and a few adults had gathered on a driveway on the edge of Harrison Park, ruled by Pomona's notorious North Side gang. A large garage door was about to be used as a movie screen for a Victory Outreach film, *The*

Duke of Earl. The plot involves two neighborhood gangs fighting for control of street drug traffic, battling each other for respect and territory. Members of Victory Outreach of San Jose served as the cast and provided the musical score. The film is loaded with gunfire and bloody deaths, including children caught in the crossfire.

But suddenly that night, the gunfire was real. The audience was ambushed from behind by pistol shots fired indiscriminately into the crowd. People screamed. Street-wise teens hit the ground. A sixth-grade boy named Alfred Hernandez flopped to the ground, hit in

Families Held Hostage

When I ran drug and alcohol rehabilitation centers in New York, California, and North Carolina, I always was deeply touched by family members who brought troubled sons and daughters to me. The families were desperate—they were hurting men and women who loved their children. Some came from middle- and upper-class homes, some extremely wealthy; all were looking for any way out, for something that would help their children to change. It was unimaginably difficult.

The addicts kept their families hostage, and the whole family began to lose hope. Now I wonder why I didn't spend more time counseling with the families. These people are victimized, held hostage by their own sons or daughters. They literally don't know what to do.

I found that at least 85-90 percent of the addicts did have a home to go to. The major reason why most drug addicts don't acknowledge their problem is that they think they have a family at home, a place to turn to. Unfortunately, the family begins to lie to protect their son or daughter. The family worries, *Where is she? What is he doing?*

I honestly came to the conclusion that the desperate one who hits the bottom, the one who finally has realized that he has lost everything—his family is gone, he is forced to beg for money and food—he is the one who feels most wretched, yet he is also the one who is closest to help.

the back by a bullet, his T-shirt stained red with blood.

Voices called out in the darkness, declaring in boldness the authority of God, pleading the protecting blood of Jesus Christ as shots continued. Then the firing stopped. In a squeal of tires, the teenage gunmen sped away.

Witnesses will never forget the horrifying muzzle flashes and the quick pop-pop-pop of gunfire. Four spectators were wounded, including Alfred. All four were rushed to hospitals. Meanwhile, word sped through the Victory Outreach churches. Within minutes, prayer warriors lifted their voices in faith. "Lord, save the life of that little boy," they pled.

Their prayers were answered. Sixth-grader Alfred was treated and released; so were the others.

And a few days later when a sixteen-year-old suspect was arrested for the shootings, Victory Outreach workers were dispatched to the jail to talk to him about Jesus.

This is Ministry with a capital "M."

A PHILOSOPHY THAT WORKS

What makes Victory Outreach go? A strong, shared philosophy of ministry undergirds all the sites, wherever they are. For example, Victory Outreach strongly encourages its members to get off welfare. This is one of its strongest philosophical planks. "You just can't get back your dignity when you are demeaned by the welfare system," says Sonny. "It is such a remarkable thing to see what happens when people whose families have been on public assistance for generations start working, saving their money, tithing to their church, buying their own homes, and holding their heads high. They shed the shame that comes with being on welfare and having social workers barge into their homes and dictate how they live and discipline their children."

Members are also strongly encouraged to hold children accountable for their actions. Biblical principles are taught: loving, firm parental discipline, which may include spanking in extreme circumstances, delivered with love and quite often accompanied by tears on the part of both parent and child. When delivered calmly, wisely, and with love, discipline results in true repentance, not resentment.

"Jesus spelled out the prime responsibility of the church," says Sonny, "when he said, 'Go ye into the whole world and preach the gospel to every creature.' That includes the dangerous streets of America's war zones and its disintegrating families. There are some people who put evangelism last, but we try to keep it first and forever before us. God has called us to evangelize the inner city. He has called us all to be disciples in the inner city and to make disciples in the inner city."

This is the special calling of Victory Outreach. All members are taught to evangelize within their spheres of influence. They are taught that they are called by God to win others to him in the worst parts of the most violence-wracked cities, that they are to be disciples in the inner city—that Christianity is a lifestyle, not a hobby.

So what does it mean to disciple somebody? "It means you have to love them," says Sonny. "You can't just pray for their salvation, then shake their hand and wish them a 'happy rest of their life.'"

In inner-city evangelism, this means the street evangelist may have to help the new believer find somewhere to live—which could mean bringing him home. The discipler must be willing to spend quality time with a convert and be completely honest with him or her—giving the disciple a realistic view of the believer's life and what a Christian relationship really is.

Winning someone to Jesus may mean showing them your changed lifestyle day to day. It may mean personal sacrifice. It certainly means caring for the person, not regarding him or her as a project or the object of Christian duty. That is one reason that soul-winning cannot be left up to the clergy alone. No pastor can spend the quality time with every convert that is needed. Ordinary, everyday Christians must make themselves available to newcomers.

"You must be available," says Sonny. "You must pray with them. You must spend time with them. That may mean telephoning them, listening to their needs, affirming and encouraging them—and confronting them with their unconfessed sin if you discern it. You should expect to share your life with them—even giving them things you have that they need after you seek the Lord's wisdom in the matter. You cannot merely minister to their spiritual needs.

"Luke 2:52 shows that Jesus grew in four different areas: wisdom, stature, in favor with God, and in favor with men. What does that mean for new Christians? They need ministry to grow mentally, physically, spiritually, and socially. The discipler must spend time with the disciple. That means going to church together, eating out together, exercising together, shopping together, traveling together, praying together, witnessing together, going to events together, and studying together—just to name a few. A new Christian can never be expected just to go it alone. He or she needs fellowship and big doses of encouragement."

As you might expect, Victory Outreach does not shut down on Sunday afternoon only to reopen for Wednesday night prayer meeting, then sit silent again until Sunday morning church services. Instead, it is a constant hub of activity, ranging from church-sponsored afternoon sports activities to bold street outreach (which can mean rallies with megaphones and live music or just tract-passing on busy sidewalks).

Many Victory Outreach members say they found themselves in gangs in search of family and a sense of belonging that they could not find elsewhere. Although they are now drug-free and sober and law-abiding, they continue to need that feeling of family—of connectedness—and they say they find it at Victory Outreach. There too they find the dignity that is so critical. Even the heroin-shooting prostitutes on the street or the winos sleeping in the alley yearn for dignity, to be able to hold their heads high, to be proud of themselves, to know they are loved, and that through the power of Jesus Christ they are going to make it. Victory Outreach helps them find that dignity.

The congregations of Victory Outreach serve as extended families where food is shared, hand-me-down clothing is passed around, job opportunities are publicized, and where mothers of small children care for the tots of those who must work outside the home.

BUT WHO'S ON STAFF?

When one first sees the large work force at Victory Outreach, the impression may be gained that every convert goes on the church payroll. Each congregation seems to have multiple directors of this, managers of that, staff supervisors of this, coordinators of whatever—making it appear that the church is one enormous make-work project.

But look a little deeper and you will find that virtually everyone is a volunteer. Enormous pride is taken in receiving meaningful titles and the responsibility that goes with them. Delegation of authority is the lifeblood of the church's management system. People take their jobs seriously and answer to a volunteer superior if their job is done indifferently.

Yet noticeably absent is any authoritarian "discipleship" system often seen in other religious movements. If you're an usher, you receive instruction and guidance on how to usher—not mandates on how to raise your children, buy a home, or whether you may move from the area. People stay and get involved in amazing numbers for one primary reason: They are loved.

It's the greatest motivator in the world.

There is a definite progression of service opportunities at Victory Outreach. "We start off anybody who comes to Jesus at the end of the chain of command," says Sonny. "We call this the 'Entry Point' level. We talk to them and find out if they are a new Christian, a non-Christian searcher, if they are transferring from another church, if they are in need of rehabilitation, and so forth.

"Second, we work with them in what we call the 'Identification Process,' discovering their talents and gifts and finding out if they have a calling from the Lord. We do this in Level I of our Wednesday night *Challenge to Ministry* course.[2]

"Third, they go on to Level II, 'Training and Development,' in which we try to equip each person according to their leading and their skills.

"Finally, those people who express a desire to go into full-time ministry, who are accountable, who are flexible, and who are broken before the Lord—they go on into Level III of training, preparing for satellite ministry, starting new churches."

No one goes into Level III to get rich, however. Pastors of new Victory Outreach congregations generally live at the edge of poverty, while staffers—including the directors of the rehabs—usually receive only room and meals. In November of 1994 I visited Pastor Mark Garcia of the South Central L.A. Victory Outreach ministry and learned that he had just moved into a house after vacating an older apartment building a few blocks away. His former downstairs neighbors were also living with him at the time of my visit—because the previous week a carbon monoxide leak in the apartment had killed the neighbor couple's children and forced them to move out.

MINISTRY ON THE EDGE

Pastors of new churches move their families into the nastiest sections of the war zones of our biggest cities, in places where few churches ever venture and where nobody has ever heard of them. There, they go out into the darkest alleys and meanest needle parks and find drug addicts and criminals who will give what's left of their devastated lives to Jesus, then come home and move in with the pastor's family.

Vince Soliz and Paco Alvarez are both former gang members who now serve the Lord through Victory Outreach. Their stories are not at all unusual.

Vince was a third-generation gang member whose father died of an overdose and whose mother still gets high. His brother was sent to jail at age seventeen and isn't due out until the year 2025. Another brother was just released. The thirty-one-year-old Vince was saved at age twenty-three and today works with at-risk kids through a continuation high school in Whittier, California, as well as serving with Victory Outreach. At the time of our visit, Vince had an eighteen-year-old "tagger" (a gang graffiti spray-painter) living in his home. The young man was "out of control," according to Vince, but is now involved at church and is back in high school.

"He needs a lot of encouragement," says Vince. "It takes a long time." Vince is praying that God would move on his city, not only in the church but also in the community.

"These kids need someone out there who will tell them they can make it," Vince says. "My goal for the guys I work with is that they reach their potential through Jesus Christ."

Pastor Paco came from a home in which both parents were drug dealers. His mom was shot six times and lost use of an arm; a cousin died in that attack. Years later Paco himself was stabbed twenty-one times, run over by a "low rider" and left for dead. Every major organ in his body was perforated in that attack, yet he lived.

"It was an angel of God always watching over me," he says. Paco has a younger brother doing forty years in prison for triple murder, while his own eldest son spent seven years behind bars. Paco shakes his head as he recalls dressing up that son in gang clothing from the moment he was born. But it was the only life Paco knew until he found Jesus.

Paco has done time in Soledad prison, San Quentin, and a few others. He became heavily involved in heroin at age sixteen and remembers taking a gun to school every day. He distinctly recalls the day when he first walked into juvenile hall. "I believed I was destined for it," he says. "That day I beat up my cellmate."

One day Paco ran into a person whom he knew had been "messed up." The man told him Jesus could turn his life around and convinced Paco to come to Victory Outreach. So on a Sunday night in 1979 that's just what he did—and right after the service on his way home, he was stabbed twenty-one times and left for dead. He didn't return to Victory Outreach for eleven years.

But in December of 1990 Paco Alvarez turned over his life to God. He plunged into the ministry at Victory Outreach, and at the time of our meeting, four years later, he was in charge of a new outreach in Boyle Heights. "God called me to preach the gospel to gang members," Paco says, and in his neighborhood he has plenty of opportunity to fulfill his calling. His church runs three rehabs, two in the heart of gang territory. The ministry had been fiercely opposed by the gangs until three days before our visit, when Paco says his first breakthrough took place. Now opposition has lessened and the church is getting known more and more in the neighborhood, especially through an 800-number that has been set up for people in trouble. Ninety percent of Paco's congregation are gang members or former gang members.

"My job is to tell them about Jesus Christ," Paco says. "We want to be a launching-out church, to reach people, teach them, and then launch them out into the world—to the ghettos, the projects, and the barrios."

One new ministry for Victory Outreach is the brainchild of pastor Mark Garcia of the South Central L.A. church. The "24/7

Lofty—But Reachable—Goals

The "24/7 Youth Gang Center" in South Central Los Angeles has seven goals, which I believe are worth reproducing in full:

1. To provide services which will redirect gang-oriented youth to activities which benefit the youth and the community.
2. To increase communication between gang elements, community, and social agencies.
   A. Network with probation and parole officers, authorities, juvenile halls, camps, and placement homes.
   B. Reinforce network already built with the LAPD [Los Angeles Police Department] and the sheriff's department.
   C. Network with judges, probation officers, attorneys, immigration, social workers, politicians, and business.
   D. Network with parks and recreation centers, and community-based organizations.
3. To provide gang, drug, and alcohol prevention and intervention counseling, education, and support groups.
   A. Parenting classes, peer counseling, mentoring gang workers, and after-school tutoring.
   B. Crisis intervention for depression/suicide, teen pregnancies.
   C. Drug and alcohol recovery, overcomers (12-step) rap/ support group, and health education.

continued on facing page

Youth Gang Center" recently opened next to the church's sanctuary, a former four-hundred-seat movie theater. The center is "a multiracial, multicultural gang prevention and intervention program providing services designed to positively influence the lives of youth in four areas: developmentally, emotionally, socially, and spiritually."

The center includes an after-school alternatives program, a twenty-four-hour hotline, and weekly activities which target hard-core gang members and troubled youth in schools, business areas, parks, and drug-infested neighborhoods. Through partnering with parents, ex-gang members, mentors, and community-based organizations of mutual purpose, the center's goal is to inspire and instill in

---

4. To act as a referral center for the community at large and provide community awareness presentations by law enforcement officials (when available).
5. Activities:
   A. Graffiti removal program.
   B. To provide transportation to and from special events. Visit amusement parks, sports events, concerts, picnics, Bar-B-Qs, bonfires, fishing trips, outings, plays/skits, Youth Explosions, movies/video nights. Multicultural activities to include dignity in ethnic and racial roots, and unity in diversity. Urban awareness—self-defense.
   C. To provide summer programs, jobs, performing arts.
   D. Feed the homeless and visit convalescent centers.
6. Radical evangelism, Continuous Aggressive Recruitment. 24-hour hotline: 1-800-247-GANG.
   A. To provide gang workers for Continuous Aggressive Recruitment.
   B. Inner-city outreach, targeting gang-infested areas one on one, gang rallies, plays, concerts, dramas, city-wide crusades.
7. Follow-up sources/procedure:
   A. Youth activities registration sheets; Gang Center sign-ins, follow-up cards, background information sheet.
   B. Visitations: home visits, hospital visits, youth authority facilities, camps, jails, referrals.
   C. Phones, letters, visitation, transportation.

these youth a desire to fulfill their potential in life "with a sense of dignity, belonging, and destiny."

As you can see, Victory Outreach takes its mission statement seriously. It intends to make a difference where God has planted it—in the heart of the most needy neighborhoods in America. If you truly want to serve the Lord, you can find an appropriate place at Victory Outreach. There's room for everybody to be involved.

READY TO SERVE? TAKE YOUR PICK

The roster of ministries within the La Puente church almost boggles the mind. There are ministries for practically any group that you can imagine, scores of ministries targeted to meet the needs of the fortunate people touched by this Christ-centered church.[3]

Yet Sonny is not satisfied.

"I look at all of it and I say it's still not enough," said Sonny. "There are still other ministries that God wants to raise up. And you know how God raises up ministries? By putting a burden on an individual's heart. All of a sudden he gives you the flash! Boom! An idea! And if he gives you a divinely inspired idea, you begin to notice the need and feel a burden on your heart—and begin to yearn to be able to meet that need. There are still needs in this church that need to be met. God wants to raise up people to meet those needs. That's what's exciting about serving the Lord in a vital, dynamic, working church. When people are working for God, when they are being edified, when the needs of God's people are being met—it is exciting!"

But don't talk to Sonny about pew-sitters. You're likely to get a lecture on biblical service.

"Doing nothing is wrong," he says with fierce conviction. "If you are not doing anything, if you're just sitting there, there is something wrong with your Christianity. If you are not doing anything, your Christianity is not complete. I'm not saying you're not saved; I'm not questioning your love for God—but I can tell you that you're not functioning as a Christian should function, nor functioning as the Bible tells you to."

THE VISION OF VICTORY OUTREACH

All effective leaders know that in order for a project to be successful, there has to be a vision. Sonny and Julie Arguinzoni are no exception to this rule.

Early on in his ministry, smack in the middle of a sermon that he had toiled over, Sonny put aside the three points of his carefully prepared notes and looked out over his congregation of perhaps one hundred ex-addicts and recovering substance abusers.

"You may think you're nothing," he said, speaking words that the Lord was putting in his heart. "We may be nobodies in the eyes of the world, but God will use us. He'll use us to preach his Word and be a witness to the power of the Spirit. We are the people who will take cities for God. God is going to raise up prophets and teachers from this congregation. He's going to raise you up, put his hands on you, and send you all over the world."

Julie especially remembers his words, "all over the world."

"I was wondering how next week's bills were going to be paid," she recalled. "Now, here my husband was planning to unleash these baby Christians on the world. *They're all on welfare,* I thought to myself, *and he's planning to take on the world!*"

But Sonny's vision for Victory Outreach—a vision inspired by God, not through mere human effort—took root and grew. Today, Victory Outreach churches are all over the globe. Sonny is well aware that nothing he would have tried to do or achieve could have succeeded without that vision of what God desired and expected of him.

WHAT'S YOUR VISION?

It is a truism that if you are feeling the call of God to minister to the hurting people around you, then you had better have a vision for it. It is crucial to serve God out of a sure vision, and Christians must understand what God's vision is for them. We all must be sure that some ministry we have in mind is God's plan for us, not some bright idea that we've cooked up out of our desire to hear from God.

Vision is a mission received from God through which our strengths and goals will be divinely directed. It is seeing more than what our eyes can perceive and our minds can imagine.

A vision is not the same as human goals, plans, or programs. It is not human desire to direct others to fulfill human wishes. Nor is it doing that which we desire for ourselves. Instead, it is a "big picture" of that which God wishes us to do. This cannot be the result of emotionalism or wishful thinking, but instead is a deep understanding of the will of God relating to something specific the Lord wants us to do. A true vision must manifest the power and comfort of God and will be confirmed by others.

God doesn't reserve visions only for men like Sonny. God has a vision for you, too. With all my heart, I want you, like Sonny, to be able to obey God. I urge you to present yourself to God, sincerely seeking his will for you. God desires leaders who will seek his vision for their lives.

We serve a great and mighty God, and he has a vision for you, just as surely as he did for Sonny Arguinzoni. If you will be obedient, he will let you run with that vision. And running can make all the difference to a world that's paralyzed in sin.

> Do you not know that in a race all the runners run, but only one gets the prize? Run in such a way as to get the prize. Everyone who competes in the games goes into strict training. They do it to get a crown that will not last; but we do it to get a crown that will last forever.   **1 Corinthians 9:24-25**

The crowns are out there. One of them has your name on it. Now it's your job to seek God earnestly and discover what vision he has in mind for you.

And then *run!*

A Little Exercise Never Hurt Anybody

In order to help you run effectively, I'd like to close this chapter with a few questions to help you sort out an appropriate response. Read and then thoughtfully answer the following questions:

1. What vision is the Lord giving me for my life? Do others agree with this vision?

2. How has the Lord equipped me, specifically, for works of service? How am I especially gifted?

3. Do I know the youth in my neighborhood? Why or why not?

4. In what ways might I serve youth in my neighborhood? Is there something not being done that ought to be? Am I qualified to do something about it? Why or why not?

5. Is there anything my family can do to assist at-risk youth in our town? If so, what? Who is doing such work already? Would it be possible for us to partner with them? If so, how? If not, why not?

6. What is my church community doing to respond to the youth emergency? How aware is my church of the problems? What recent incidents in our neighborhood should alert us to the dimensions of the problem? With whom can I discuss our church's response?

7. What churches in our town would make good "partners" to address the youth emergency? What churches are doing a good job of addressing the problems? What resources do they need? How could my own church provide some assistance?

8. What one thing could I do *now* as a personal response to the Code Blue? How can I participate in what God wants to do in the lives of young people in my neighborhood and community?

CHAPTER 7

Save Our Cities

S ometimes, it takes a little person to bring big hope. I had been speaking to a large crowd at a crusade in San Antonio, Texas. After I invited members of the audience to come forward and receive Jesus, about three hundred to four hundred kids responded—some crying so hard they were gasping for air. I was especially moved by one little African-American girl.

I had begun to pray for those who came forward and I was hugging one little Mexican boy and this little black girl. In the middle of my prayer I broke down. I couldn't help myself! It was impossible not to see the young Nicky Cruz in all these precious children. Old, painful memories came rushing back:

- the love I so desperately wanted but never had;

- the longing for a hug and a kiss;

- the intense ache in my soul for just one adult to show me genuine love.

I simply couldn't handle the flood of emotions that engulfed me, and I broke down and wept.

At just that point, this adorable little girl began hugging my leg and patting my back in an effort to reassure me. "It's all right," she said with childlike empathy and gentleness. "Don't cry—you're going to make it."

And then a miracle happened. Hope flooded my soul once again. Without a doubt, it was one of the greatest moments I've ever enjoyed in all my years of serving the Lord. And it took a little girl from deep poverty to bring me back to hope.

WHERE IS HOPE?

No one can survive without hope. I believe it was Norman Cousins who once said something along the lines of "Mankind can surivive a month without food, a few days without water, a few minutes without air, but not one second without hope."

The disciples certainly knew the importance of hope. As fishermen, they couldn't live without it. While they couldn't see the fish below their boat, they had to hope they'd be there. Otherwise, they knew they were in for a long day and a short paycheck.

One day their hopes were being sorely tested. They had fished all day yet had caught nothing. Then a rather strange fellow—no fisherman, although some thought he might be the Messiah—gave them some perplexing instructions. They weren't sure about what he told them to do, but already they had seen there was something different about this man. Here's how Luke describes the story:

> When he [Jesus] finished speaking, he said to Simon, "Put out into deep water, and let down the nets for a catch." Simon answered, "Master, we've worked hard all night and haven't caught anything. But because you say so, I will let down the nets."
>
> **Luke 5:4-5**

Now, try to put yourself into Simon's sandals for a moment. You've worked all night, straining and sweating and toiling over ancient nets that should have been replaced long ago. You've heaved those frayed old fish-catchers over the side time and again, allowed them to sink where you had hoped was a big school of fish, and then slowly and agonizingly dragged them back over the gunwales of your boat.

Your muscles ache. You've probably cramped up more than once. You're famished, you're exhausted, you're angry and testy and frustrated all at once. Especially frustrated! Because no matter how many times you've repeated the futile procedure, you've come up empty. No big school of fish. No big fish. No fish at all. In fact, not even a minnow. You've worked as hard as you've ever toiled in your life, but all you have to show for it is a growling belly and a pile of seaweed. So what do you do? You give up.

You can't blame Peter for doing exactly that. With a deep sigh, he hauled in his nets, stored them away, hoisted his sail, and headed for land. By the time this conversation between Jesus and Peter occurred, he was already on shore, safe and dry... and now Jesus was asking him to go out into the deep waters again!

THE BIRTH OF A NEW HOPE

You know what? I know exactly how Simon Peter must have felt. My staff and I at Nicky Cruz Outreach were on "shore" doing our normal crusades in churches and auditoriums and ministering whenever we could to gang members and drug addicts. Financially we were keeping our heads just above water, we were seeing God move in our services, and everything seemed just fine.

Then the Lord began speaking to me about returning to the inner city with a new kind of evangelism, a new hope. This would represent a major turning point for me. Yet I strongly felt the Lord calling me back to the streets on a more full-time basis, to reclaim our cities for God with tough, aggressive, in-your-face evangelism.

With God's voice ringing in my ears, I decided to accept fewer and fewer international speaking engagements in order to concentrate on the increasing gang epidemic of our country. I realized we are at a pivotal place in the history of our nation and that young people are going to play the central role. Drugs are out of control in the public schools. The gangs are trying to run the schools, and school officials are asking us for help. Hope is desperately needed but nowhere to be seen. So we moved ahead with the new focus.

As soon as we began to pursue this calling, however, two things happened: Financially our account went down to a point so low that we had only enough funds to pay the next week's worth of bills; and secondly we were flooded with requests by churches to come and hold crusades. Now understand, we have always depended upon these church crusades to bring in the donations which meet our budget.

And now God was asking us to "put out into the deep water"! What could we do? The only thing possible: "Simon Peter, wait for us!"

With a prayer for divine strength and courage, we committed ourselves to obeying the Lord's command. We invested our time, energy, and resources into seeing the inner cities of America evangelized. We were all in a boat, we pushed out from the safety of the shore, and we said, "Let's cross to the other side."

CATCHING THE WIND OF THE SPIRIT

We even christened the boat! We named it the "Save Our City" campaign and we have aggressive plans to take it—and hope along with it—to several targeted cities across the United States.

Every major venture like this one needs a mission statement. So here's ours: "To work in an urban environment with youth of all economic and ethnic backgrounds who are caught in a downward spiral of violence, drug abuse, and gang activity, and introduce them back into the mainstream of society by challenging them to a fundamental and permanent change spiritually, and by investing in their leadership development, equipping them to live healthy, productive lives."

In the Save Our City invasions we directly address the needs of the people by challenging them to a lifetime commitment of change and growth. Those who respond to this challenge are given the opportunity to receive follow-up counseling, coordinated through local outreach centers. Accurate records are kept, ensuring that these people's needs are being addressed. Depending on the severity of their needs, they are directed and encouraged to attend a church of their choice, enter a rehab program, or both, the goal being to train them and develop their leadership capabilities so that they will in turn become proactive participants in reaching out to others among their peers.

We strongly encourage these individuals to finish their high school education and pursue further training in college or at a vocational institution. In each city we look into the possibility of securing corporate sponsorship for scholarships, job training programs, and internships. Concerted efforts are made to network at-risk kids with churches, families, and businesses.

In a nutshell, that's what we're up to these days. So how is it going, you ask? Has our ship caught the mighty wind of the Spirit? Are we sailing—or just drifting aimlessly, anxiously hoping for a whiff of a divine breeze?

Friends, can you spell "nor'easter"?

Right now, in dozens of cities across this country, we are organizing churches and groups to work together in sponsoring crusades in the depths of the inner city. Already we have seen Christians from all denominations unite and join in standing up for the gospel and in reaching out to the young people of their communities.

We are seeing genuine miracles take place in many cities. Support is being showered on these crusades by city officials, public high schools, and police and civic organizations.

But as great as our initial successes have been, now is not the time to celebrate. The biggest mistake we could make is to rejoice over these small victories and cease being prayerful and on the offensive. I thank God for these open doors—but I won't fall for the smoke screen that the battle is over.

After all, it's hardly begun.

LOVE AND REBIRTH

A 1992 crusade in Wichita, Kansas, was instrumental in convincing me of the need to follow through on this new track.

At that time, Wichita had been in the national news with frequent, hostile conflicts over the abortion issue. Wichita is a city of about 300,000 people and is home to about fifty-five active gangs, with gang membership on the rise. Homicides were up, as were drug sales and satanic activity.

The city held a "Freedom March" several days before our crusade. Concerned citizens from the Asian, black, Hispanic, and white communities marched from their respective areas of Wichita and converged on a downtown park for a rally. The mayor, the state attorney general, and the city police chief all showed up at the meeting and stated publicly that, in their opinion, the only hope for Wichita was God!

A good crowd of about thirty-five hundred attended the crusade itself. Many gang members, drug addicts, and street kids came, and nearly five hundred went forward at the altar call afterward! And all this despite stiff "competition" the evening of the meeting.

In another part of the city that night, a popular rapper known for lyrics filled with violence, profanity, and sexually explicit words also was making an appearance. I don't know what kind of crowd he attracted, but I do know I got a shock the next day when I opened up the local newspaper, *The Wichita Eagle.*

The paper's critic surprisingly gave our crusade a better review than he did the rap concert! The writer contrasted our meeting with the rapper's performance and pointed out the key differences between the two events. The headline stated: "Performances by Ice T, Cruz span the spectrum." It wasn't too hard to see which end of the spectrum the critic appreciated most. "While rap singer Ice T and gang member-turned-evangelist Nicky Cruz covered similar ground—despair and anger among urban youth—their messages were poles apart," he wrote. "Ice T's raps were full of violence and vulgarity, and Cruz's message was one of love and rebirth."

Love and rebirth—this secular journalist got it on the nose! The Save Our City campaigns are all about how love and rebirth can overcome violence and vulgarity. We don't have to wallow in our sin. We don't have to grope around in the kingdom of darkness. We don't have to play the devil's game or fall into Satan's trap. We have the light of the gospel to blaze a trail for us into the loving and waiting arms of God Almighty! Wichita heard that message loud and clear, and for that we were overjoyed.

But we couldn't stop with Wichita. Not if we were to follow the example of the Master. As Matthew 9:35-36 tells us, "Jesus went through *all* the towns and villages... preaching the good news of the kingdom.... When he saw the crowds, he was moved with compassion for them" [emphasis added].

We knew that this message of hope in Jesus—and *only* in Jesus—had to be taken to "all the towns and villages" and all the major cities of this hemorrhaging country of ours. Jesus was moved with compassion for the people of his day when he saw they were like sheep without a shepherd. So many lost sheep! Such deep despair! The Lord felt compelled to go out and search for those lost sheep of his. Today, he calls us to do the same, for there are even more lost sheep now than there were then.

A lot of them are in Houston, Texas. So that's where we launched the maiden voyage of our Save Our City invasions.

THE WORST OF THE WORST

Months before our first Save Our City campaign, I was invited to speak at a large, inner-city Houston high school. A mandatory assembly had been arranged by the substance abuse monitor, who is a Christian. The monitor had been working closely with many of the gang leaders and drug dealers in the school and was making a lot of progress with them. (Adrian, whose story I told earlier, was one of these kids.) These young men and women were opening up to the monitor and after months of laboring, mutual trust had been established.

Two weeks before I spoke at this high school, there had been a gang-related murder. No less than thirty-three active gangs operate in and around the school. The top three gangs in the area all have strong presences in the high school itself. Normally they are at war with each other, but before I arrived, two of the gangs had formed a truce in order to go after the president of the third gang, a young man who had overstepped his turf by breaking one of the unspoken laws of the gangs. One night, leaders of the two allied gangs went after this boy, kidnapped him, and threw him in a car. They fatally shot him in the head and threw his body out of their moving car!

The gang leaders who carried out the execution were at the assembly, although I did not know it at the time. I cannot tell you how deeply it grieves my heart to know that there are sixteen- and seventeen-year-olds who are this violent and who have such little regard for human life. As we have recalled throughout this book, it is no longer uncommon to read of boys and girls as young as nine and ten who are committing similar acts of revenge... or worse.

During the assembly, I first spoke for forty minutes to the entire student body. Then I was asked to do a second assembly with "the worst of the worst," 175 of the most notorious drug dealers and gang members in the school. I was given complete liberty to speak about anything I chose. I was free not only to share about my past, but also to tell about the power of Jesus that changed my life and turned me from a vicious gang warlord into a minister of the gospel of Jesus Christ. Can you imagine that—in a public high school, somebody talking about God? And not getting read the riot act because of it? But that is how desperate some of our school officials are becoming. They have no power to slow down the evil, and they'll invite in anyone who has shown they know where such a power can be found.

At the second assembly I spoke for forty-five minutes, and afterward talked with many of the kids individually. I also took along twenty ex-gang leaders and drug dealers who were able to minister to many of the students one on one.

A few weeks later, more than forty Houston churches from all denominations joined together to fight for the spiritual survival of Houston. I spoke at four Houston high school assemblies to more than twenty-two hundred students.

In four evening crusades, we ministered to many gang members and drug dealers, and more than five hundred people gave their lives to Jesus. The churches are continuing to work together, and the mayor's office, the police department, and the high schools are anxious to partner with anyone who can help make a positive difference in their troubled city.

Death in Chicago

September and October of 1994 were bad months for Chicago, "the city of broad shoulders." It needed those shoulders that year, because a lot of people there were crying on them.

First, consider the sad and tragic story of Robert "Yummy" Sandifer. On August 28, a Sunday evening, eleven-year-old Robert had pulled an automatic pistol and sprayed a street corner with bullets, killing fourteen-year-old Shavon Dean. Three nights later he himself was murdered, shot twice in the back of the head. He was found lying in a bloody mud puddle under a pedestrian viaduct less than a mile from his home. Two teenage brothers, members of Robert's gang, the Black Disciples, were charged with his murder. Police said Robert had been killed for "botching" an assassination attempt; when Shavon was mistakenly killed, he had brought too much "heat" down on the rest of the gang.

It turned out that Robert had first been arrested for armed robbery when he was nine years old, had a teenage mom who was abusive, a dad in jail, and had been raised (along with his siblings) by his grandmother. The year prior to his death he was made a ward of the state because of neglect.[51]

Countless strangers attended Robert's funeral. Mothers and grandmothers skipped work to take their own children and grandchildren to see what a life of violence leads to. "I brought my grandson here to see what can happen in gangs," said Catherine Wilder, forty-seven. "That's a baby in there, and I'm scared to death for mine."

One report said that "the young men who fight and die in the city's gang wars, and even eighteen-year-old veterans who, like Javon Goodlow, say they have quit the gangs in fear and disgust, do not harbor much hope that Robert's death will make a difference, at least not until more alternatives exist to the streets and loveless homes. 'Half the kids don't care if they live or die,' Goodlow said Wednesday after he went to view Robert's body, even though he had never met the boy. 'Their mamas don't care about them. The police and society don't care. It's just one less boy to worry about.... It's hard to live in this world... I be afraid to go to school. They do the same thing there. They sell drugs. They shoot. They die!"

Chicago police said the Black Disciples, a gang of five thousand

continued on page 151

JESUS COMES TO BEXAR COUNTY JUVENILE CENTER

Houston was officially our first Save Our City invasion, but in a real sense it was only preliminary to what was about to happen. San Antonio was chosen as the next community to experience this more aggressive type of crusade, and it would turn out to be a blessing far beyond anything I had imagined.

Prior to the September 1993 crusade, I visited San Antonio to make preparations for the invasion and had the opportunity to speak at Bexar County Juvenile Center in San Antonio. On this hot, muggy Texas day there were eighty-seven boys and girls who gathered to hear my testimony. They had to be separated into two groups to keep rival gang factions apart.

As I told them about my experience in an abusive family, my rejection at an early age, being a gang leader, and my involvement in crime, drug abuse, and violence, I could tell many of them had suffered through similar horrors. Although these kids were young—all between eleven and seventeen years of age—many of them were vicious. Nearly 70 percent of my audience was incarcerated for violent crimes ranging from aggravated assault with a deadly weapon to murder. Seventeen were being held for murder and capital murder.

I poured out my heart to these young people, telling them of the love of Jesus and how he had the power to give them new lives, free from bitterness and rage and violence and instead filled with peace and love and acceptance. I told them frankly of my life before Christ and what it became by his grace after I accepted him as my Savior and my Lord. I told them that whatever he had done for me, he could do for them, too—and that he longed with all his heart to do so. But it was up to them.

Before I asked anyone to respond to an altar call, however, I wanted to make sure that everyone understood what they were being asked to do. I told them that if they asked Jesus into their hearts, nothing about their external situation would change—becoming a Christian was not a fast way out of jail. They would still have to face criminal charges. The only difference would be that Jesus would be there with them, going through everything by their side. And that is a huge, huge difference!

members, often uses adolescents as triggermen. Twenty percent of the gang's members are under age thirteen.[52] "Yummy" himself had bragged about his affiliation with the Black Disciples since he was ten, while the brothers charged with his murder also had become members at ten.

Editorials in newspapers across the country expressed both outrage and sadness over the tragedy. Typical was this comment:

> If the short, miserable life of Robert Sandifer, the slain eleven-year-old Chicago gangster, is offered as an object lesson, then the root is family disintegration, child abuse, and neglect. Child-welfare records say his body bore cigarette burns and belt marks before he was three. Fellow gang members killed him, it's said, for attracting too much police attention by botching an ordered assassination with the accidental killing of a fourteen-year-old girl, Shavon Dean.... A society that fails to protect its young can expect to pay heavily when children grow into violent adults.[53]

As tragic as Yummy's story was, even this was not the end of the agony for Chicago. One month later, two boys, ages ten and eleven, were charged with shoving a five-year-old to his death from a fourteenth-floor window because he wouldn't steal candy for them.

Eric Morris died of massive internal injuries after a desperate struggle at the window of a vacant apartment in the Ida B. Wells housing project on Chicago's South Side. His eight-year-old brother, Derrick, fought with the two older boys as they tried to push Eric out the window. Derrick pulled his brother back from the brink as he dangled from the window ledge, but he lost his grip when one of the older boys bit Derrick's arm.

"It's truly mind-boggling," said Kay Hanlon, an assistant state's attorney prosecuting the case. "Every day you think you've seen as bad as it's ever going to get here and something like this happens." "Our victims are getting younger and our offenders are getting younger," added police Commander Charles Smith, who led the investigation of Eric's death.[54]

At the time of the murder, the ten-year-old suspect was under a court order to be confined to his house after being sentenced for unlawful use of a weapon. When the suspects appeared before a judge at a preliminary hearing, they were barely tall enough to peer over the judge's desk. Both boys said their fathers were in prison.[55]

When I finally asked these young people to accept Jesus, sixty-six of them raised their hands, came forward, and knelt on the gym floor. As I prayed for them, my mind raced back to when I was still in the gangs and in and out of jail. Many of them cried, asking God to forgive them and come into their hearts. We stayed and prayed with them for a few moments and gave each one a copy of *Run, Baby, Run.*

Several days later, Chaplain Skip Good of the detention center relayed to us the following highlights:

- One of the girls who gave her heart to Jesus had been a lesbian. Another girl, a self-proclaimed satanist, asked for a Bible.

- Two girls from rival gangs (Crips and Bloods) hugged each other and prayed.

- Some kids said they were glad that they got busted so they could hear about Jesus.

- One eleven-year-old boy who was in for three counts of capital murder and drug dealing went forward to receive Jesus.

This deeply moving service confirmed to me once more the tremendous need that exists in our inner cities. These kids are violent and they have little or no respect for life or authority. Yet they still respect God! They are hungry and open to the gospel. This is why we are going back to the streets with our Save Our City invasions.

ST. TONY NEEDS SALVATION TOO

For our first major Save Our City event in San Antonio, we planned to take one hundred former gang members and addicts to the ghettos three weeks before the crusades. They were to go door-to-door, promoting the events and sharing how Jesus changed their lives.

I say we *planned* to take one hundred former gang members and addicts, because when the time came for the crusade, we actually had almost double that number! This mighty team of men and women assisted in publicity and also trained volunteers on how to relate to and counsel drug addicts and gang members. One of these valued volunteers was Archie Archuleta, a former gang member from San Diego, who spoke of his conversion to Christianity at a Tuesday rally at city hall announcing our September crusade against drugs and gang activity.

Already we had mobilized local churches and counselors to handle the enormous task of following up on the new Christians. Dozens of churches in San Antonio offered their support, as well as business leaders, law enforcement officials, members of city government and the high schools. They told us of the desperate need in their city and were willing to do anything to see their young people reached with the love of Jesus. The mayor, Nelson W. Wolff, even wrote a letter that we could use to show other San Antonians that we were on the up-and-up:

City of San Antonio
Nelson W. Wolff
Mayor

December 28, 1992

To Whom It May Concern:

As you are well aware, today's youth and their families face traumatic and perilous conditions on a daily basis, often requiring many of the available resources from within the community. As we enter the new year, the needs of our youth and their families should become one of our greatest priorities. Coming to our city September 9-13, 1993, is Nicky Cruz, a man with a powerful message and an effective method of reaching today's youth and their families. It is imperative that we as a city support this opportunity to positively affect the youth of San Antonio.

Mr. Cruz's campaign "Save Our City" is headed locally by Rev. Wane E. Crooks, who has worked with me on issues regarding youth development. I have long been concerned for the future of our youth and believe that they need the positive influence and guidance necessary to develop into responsible adults. I strongly encourage every segment of our community to join in the all-important fight against youth crime and violence by offering whatever assistance is necessary to ensure a successful campaign in our city.

Sincerely,
Nelson W. Wolff
Mayor

We went to the battlefield with a song of praise in our mouths and a two-edged sword in our hands!

Save Our City-San Antonio was four days of outreach into some of the worst areas of the community. Our goal was to make this effort serve as a pilot project for other communities across the United States.

I want to tell you that we saw miracles, signs, and wonders in San Antonio as we ministered to the gangs! It was an uphill fight, but in the end, we saw almost two thousand give their lives to Jesus during the three weeks before the crusades, and over three thousand more accept Christ during the evening meetings!

But I'm getting ahead of myself, aren't I? Sorry, but what do you expect—I'm Latin! When it comes to my Jesus, you can't expect me to sit on my hands and drone on and on about this statistic or that statistic like some pastor from the Been-There-Done-That Church of the Nearly Dead. *Living for Jesus is exciting!*

But I do want to give you a few more details about the San Antonio Save Our City invasion. So hang on!

THE ALAMO'S OK, BUT JESUS IS BETTER

We did street-corner preaching, sidewalk drama, and classic one-on-one witnessing with dopers and gang members on the sidewalks and in the parks and on the basketball courts. We went to the barrios, to the government housing projects and into some of the roughest neighborhoods of San Antonio. We split up into two groups and handed out fliers and complimentary tickets to the evening crusade meetings.

And during the three weeks of work to promote four days of citywide rallies, close to two thousand people came to the Lord!

The first night of the rallies, Thursday, September 9, more than twelve hundred street youths and their families gathered in the pouring rain in San Antonio's Pittman-Sullivan Park to hear the gospel through me and Christian singers Linda and Steven Tavani. Linda is "Peaches" of the pop duo "Peaches and Herb," which sold more than nine million records, including the hit "Reunited." The rain subsided as I got up to speak—and more than 250 gathered at the altar afterward to give their lives to Jesus.

On Friday, more than twenty-two hundred gathered in Rosedale Park to hear the Tavanis, a twenty-minute drama, as well as a Christian rap artist. After I preached, more than four hundred responded to the altar call.

On Saturday, two lines into San Antonio's Burbank High School began forming at 4 P.M. for the 7 P.M. crusade, which featured the multi-media live drama *The Duke of Earl II*, presented by thirty former gang members and drug addicts from San Jose, California. The action-packed play and live music includes gang fighting by young actors who had participated in the real thing before they gave their hearts to Jesus. More than half the crowd could not get into the large auditorium, but waited for three hours for an encore, standing-room-only 10 P.M. performance. At the end of both performances, I spoke and hundreds streamed down the aisles to give their hearts to the Lord.

Just when we thought the crusade could get no better, when we convinced ourselves we had experienced the climax of the Lord's blessing on our four days in San Antonio, the last evening brought even more powerful results. On Sunday police officials became concerned when crowds started forming for the final event at San Antonio's Municipal Auditorium—particularly since rival gangs were eyeing each other ominously. Suspected gang members were searched by security officers before being allowed into the auditorium. Finally, after waiting in line for several hours, well over five thousand crowded the auditorium.

After another performance of *The Duke of Earl II*, I gave a brief message and then invited any who wanted to give their lives to Christ to come to the front. The first to respond to the altar call were eight boys from one gang. They prominently displayed their "colors" on their bandanas, which were draped over their shoulders. Then a half-dozen members from a rival gang stood up and walked single file onto the platform. Within minutes, seventeen hundred people had crowded in, filling the entire stage!

I can assure you that the majority of the people who crowded the platform that night were new converts, many of whom had never stepped foot in a church in their life!

All during the yearlong planning stages for this crusade, police officers had been insistent that there was no solution to San Antonio's drug- and gang-related crime problems. But after seventeen hundred street kids, gang members, and drug abusers responded to the altar call that evening, several minds were changed. "Maybe you people do have the answer," one officer told me.

One local pastor, John Hagee of Cornerstone Church, witnessed the mass of people who filled the stage at the Municipal and confessed in his newsletter, *The Cluster*, that he had seen more souls won to Christ in San Antonio in 1993 through unconventional evangelism than in all of the church-centered crusades *combined* in the past decade! In an article headlined, "Nicky Cruz Crusade Impacts S.A. Youth Gangs," he went on to say, "It burns me to the bone that the [secular] media refuses to cover a spiritual event that solves the problem of street gangs... but will give tons of print and coverage to government programs that create and sustain the problem."

MY BIGGEST SURPRISE

Do you know what surprised me the most about the crusade? After proclaiming Jesus Christ to gang members and drug abusers

Dead at the Deepest Levels

It's tragic enough that kids are killing kids every day. But the worst part of it is that many troubled youth are headed down the path of spiritual suicide. Premarital sex and abortion are two of the most common, everyday soul-killers.

Professor Elijah Anderson of the University of Pennsylvania, described as "a scrupulous and sympathetic observer of ghetto life" by *Washington Post* writer Charles Krauthammer, in 1993 released a five-year study titled "Sex Codes among Inner-City Youth." In it he reports in detail the sex-and-abandonment "game" played by boys and girls in an impoverished Philadelphia community. Krauthammer calls it "the story of family breakdown on an unprecedented scale."[S1]

Anderson himself writes:

> Casual sex with as many women as possible, impregnating one or more, and getting them to "have your baby" brings a boy the ultimate in esteem from his peers and makes him a man. But because owning up to a pregnancy goes against the peer-group ethic of "hit and run," (abandonment is the norm.)[S2]

This makes for illegitimacy rates as high as 80 percent, with intergenerational poverty and social chaos the inevitable result.[S3]

This new flood of illegitimacy prompted Charles Murray of *The Wall Street Journal* to lament that not too long ago, "America accepted as a matter of course that a free society such as ours can sustain itself only through virtue and temperance, that these values must be taught to each new generation, and that this task depends on the care and resources fostered by marriage."[S4] Yet thousands of children each year (who are not aborted) will grow up in an environment devoid of any such values.

It's amazing to me that the same culture that produces the passion of a Humane Society for animal life can be so indifferent to human life. The church of the Lord needs to get just as passionate about the worth of the human soul!

in the parks and public auditoriums of San Antonio, I admit I was more than a little startled to find myself praying at the altar with large numbers of *preteens*—little children attracted to the citywide street rallies.

These were little street kids, some as young as eight years old! I couldn't help but remember my own years on the streets of New York City, when as a young man I was caught up in the excitement of youth gang violence.

As we knelt and prayed with these little children, we saw such desperation and hopelessness in their eyes. They were looking for a way out. For many of them, this ordinarily would have meant a life of drugs, gang activity, and violent crimes. But we told them about Jesus—and they accepted the Good News with joy on their faces!

I was happy that my dear friend Sonny Arguinzoni was there with me and had the opportunity to pray with many of these children and preteens. It was a moment neither of us will ever forget.

All in all, all thanks to Jesus, I have to say the San Antonio Save Our City invasion was an amazing success. I have been so excited at the continued response of the San Antonio-area churches and businesses. Many in the suburbs have seen for the first time the horrors of gang activity and violence in their own communities, and I am convinced that we have opened a lot of eyes and that we have thrown back the darkness in a dramatic way.

But the work is far from over!

COMING INVASIONS

It is time to save our cities!

Friends, we simply must address the spirit of violence in this country. We not only need to pray, but we must act, and act despite hardships and opposition.

Leroy Favela is an example of a man who has every human reason to harbor hate and bitterness toward gang kids. His own father was gunned down in a gang shooting. Today, the forty-something Leroy runs Joy Concessions, a San Antonio company that services such major engagements as Fiesta Texas and Cinco de Mayo. He also does staging and sound for concert events in the area... and he hires gang kids to work these engagements! Sometimes he pays for his commitment to these youth. On the last night of a recent event, Leroy's van was stolen by gang members, taken for a joyride, and then burned. Yet he continues to work with these kids and is having a remarkable effect on many of them.

I tell you about Leroy because I don't want to give the impression in this chapter that what we are trying to do is all roses and no thorns. We have had our share of setbacks, and I'm sure we'll have more. But we'll continue to plow ahead because we're sure the Lord Jesus has led us to this.

Until recently we were moving ahead with plans to take the Save Our City crusade to Denver, our next-door neighbor. But in the process of the talks, some individuals there took our ideas, changed the name of the outreach to "Save Our Youth," and split the crusade. We withdrew at that point and the Denver outreach fizzled.

We have found that the biggest opposition we experience often comes not from gang members but from churches antagonistic to new ideas. Some pastors are afraid of head-on confrontation with evil; they're just not ready for it. We go into the crack houses and the alleys of the worst sections of a city, we put on programs for children in the heart of the projects. We're convinced you can't change a city with "Kumbaya, my Lord." You have to fight fire with fire.

Frankly, I don't care who gets the "credit" for helping to change the face of the inner cities of America. But if we're going to change it, we have to tackle the problems head on. That's what Save Our City is designed to do. The Save Our City campaign was created to go after the evil in this country, to snatch people from hell and usher them into heavenly places. We know there will be opposition, sometimes from unexpected places, but we have been commissioned by the Lord to move ahead.

Currently plans are under way to take the Save Our City campaign to Phoenix and Washington, D.C. A number of other cities also are being targeted.

I would like to ask you to pray and see if God might have you participate in our Save Our City crusades. This is an exciting time, but it is also scary. It is a time when kids no longer care about consequences. Every one hundred hours, more young people are killed on our streets than in the one hundred hours of ground war in Operation Desert Storm in the Persian Gulf.

Yet there is a new anointing, a fresh move of God in the inner city. God loves the crack dealer, the gangsta, the prostitute, the homeless person. God feels the frustration and anger of the urban youth—and he cares!

But do you know who is going to tell them? Do you know who has the message of hope, of change? You and I! By getting involved in some way in the Save Our City campaigns—or in some other ways that we'll talk about next—you will be helping the youth of this country who need to know there is another way besides drugs and violence.

Together we can work to change our cities for Jesus!

What Can I Do to Help Save My City?

All of us need to be thinking about what we can do to help save our own city. And perhaps one of the best places to start thinking is by asking ourselves a few key questions:

1. Am I currently praying regularly for the youth of my city? What can I do differently to make time to intercede daily for local young people?

2. Is there gang activity in my city? If so, how many gangs are there? How many youth are involved? What kind of gang activity is taking place?

3. Are any citywide Christian groups at work among the youth gangs? How might I be able to assist them or get involved with them?

4. How can I share my resources with organizations that are working to care for the youth emergency in my own city?

5. Would my city be a good candidate for a Save Our City campaign? If so, what can I do to get the ball rolling?

CHAPTER 8

Let's Get Our Hands Dirty

The young Nicky Cruz was a kid without hope. Violence was my way of life, my constant companion. I didn't expect anything out of life, and I thought I had to take by force whatever I could lay my hands on. I seldom, if ever, thought about the future. Why would I? If I wasn't sure I would even be around tomorrow, why worry about it? I knew what hopelessness is all about. I lived it every day.

That's why I understand the emotions and outrage of people in the inner city. They're sitting on a ticking time bomb of drugs, violence, gangs, and witchcraft—yet very few people seem to care.

My friends, this is a time bomb that the church *can* and *must* defuse. We cannot be satisfied with ministering only to the middle and upper classes, refusing to get our hands dirty.

I have already said that the church must become a hospital and accommodate the wounded of society. It's a joke to think that people are going to show up at the doors of the church and ask to be saved. The situation is urgent; we have no time to sit around, endlessly defining some minor point of theology or debating which denomination is closest to God's heart.

We are the ones who must defuse the bomb. We are God's bomb squad, and the clock is still ticking. It's been ticking for a long time, and time is running out.

About twenty-seven years ago, I started spilling my guts from the pulpit, predicting that an invasion of drugs was threatening to overwhelm this country and that if we didn't act immediately to stem the tide, we would all be buried under an avalanche of brutality, violence, and lawlessness. That prediction reads more like today's head-lines than I care to admit. And what I see today is more dangerous than ever. The spirit of violence already has moved from the inner cities to places where we never expected to see it.

VIOLENCE AT OUR DOORSTEP

I haven't lived in New York City for many years. For some seven-teen years now I and my family have called the beautiful little city of Colorado Springs, Colorado, "home." Founded in 1871, the city sits at the foot of Pikes Peak and was the location of a trade center for the Cripple Creek gold field. The U.S. Air Force Academy is here, snuggled against the mountains. James Dobson's Focus on the Family is also headquartered here, as are the Navigators and dozens of other evangelical missions and organizations. Oh, and do you know who else is here?

Street gangs.

Just last November, an article in the *Gazette Telegraph*, our hometown newspaper, was headlined, "Teen sentenced to life with-out parole in slaying: Victim's kin had year of 'hell.'"

The article described how eighteen-year-old Allen Lucero had been slapped with a mandatory life sentence for the first-degree murder of a seventy-one-year-old Arkansas tourist in 1993. The man, Robert Elshire, had come to Colorado Springs with his wife to prepare for his sixth Pikes Peak Ascent marathon. The evening of August 19 he was shot in the chest after leaving a drugstore. Prosecutors labeled the murder a "gang initiation."

Reporter Kathryn Sosbe recounted how Lucero began drinking alcohol when he was thirteen and was known to drink a fifth of brandy a day with several friends. He dropped out of school when he was a freshman and freely admitted to buying and selling drugs. He was an original member of a local gang, where he was known as "Little Al" or "G." Prosecutors said he was known to carry a gun and brag about his gang involvement and the crimes he had com-mitted.[1]

No, I don't live in New York anymore, but part of New York lives here. And it does wherever you live too!

But this isn't news. We all know what's been happening, and more and more of us are finally admitting it. The real question is, what can we do about it? Is there anything we *can* do?

Of course there is! We are blood-bought members of the church of Jesus Christ, and our Head is not at all in a muddle about what might be done. He's ready to give us our marching orders—if we're willing to accept them.

But It Couldn't Happen Here!

Some of us still try to find consolation in the belief that the horrible incidents regularly occupying the front pages of this nation's newspapers could happen only in the ghetto or in the barrio. Few of us want to believe such terrible things could ever happen in our communities, in our neighborhoods, and especially not to us.

But if that describes us, we're living in fantasyland. Consider the following incidents:

- After a year of bullying by a classmate, a high school freshman in rural Pennsylvania shot his enemy in the head one spring during biology class.

- Outside a brownstone in Brooklyn two weeks later, a ten-year-old boy ended an argument by plunging a steak knife into the chest of his twelve-year-old friend.

- In a central Florida subdivision, a fourteen-year-old was accused of shooting and killing his younger stepsister.

- A fifteen-year-old boy shot his forty-three-year-old mother to death as she sat in a Kansas City, Missouri, mall movie theater. "I don't know why I did it," the boy said.[S1]

- In one mid-sized city, a sixteen-year-old boy stabbed a fifteen-year-old boy to keep him from talking about another killing. A fifteen-year-old girl strangled her newborn baby. And a sixteen-year-old boy shot his mother because she wouldn't leave him and his friends alone to use drugs.[S2]

No, the youth emergency is real and it's here. Wherever we live.

SO MUCH TO DO

Even secular authorities are telling us that ordinary citizens like you and I can help stop the violence. Investigative journalist Bill Moyers has written, "There is so much we can do... we can invest our resources—public and private—in rebuilding moral and economically thriving communities. If children in the inner cities cannot live in peaceable neighborhoods, attend good schools, and find good-paying jobs, the crisis of violence will continue.

"Easy? Not at all. It will be far harder to control violence than it was to contain communism. It took forty years and four trillion dollars to win the Cold War. But violence threatens our freedom more directly than communism ever did, and we must win this struggle too. We will have to wage it on many fronts simultaneously, with programs of prevention and punishment, with new priorities and much patience, and with efforts grounded in the best possible research."[2]

A 1993 report by the American Psychological Association's Commission on Violence and Youth suggested a variety of efforts could help reverse the trend toward violence. "Psychology has a message of hope: violence is preventable," said Dr. Ronald G. Slaby, a Harvard University psychologist who was one of the commission's twelve members. "Violence is learned, and we can teach children alternatives."[3]

Hey—if *psychology* can say it has a "message of hope," what about the people of God? It is time for the church of the Lord to stand up and boldly march to the field of battle. We can't let the war be fought on a purely human plane by psychologists and psychiatrists! It was one of them, after all, who looked me in the eye many years ago and told me he saw a young man who was one step away from oblivion. "You're doomed," he told me. "There's no hope for you. And unless you change, you're on a one-way street to jail, the electric chair, and hell."

I don't blame him for saying that, of course. Because in purely human terms, I *was* on a one-way street to hell.

But who says we have to fight on purely human terms?

For though we live in the world, we do not wage war as the world does. The weapons we fight with are not the weapons of the world. On the contrary, they have divine power to demolish strongholds. We demolish arguments and every pretension that sets itself up against the knowledge of God, and we take captive every thought to make it obedient to Christ.

2 Corinthians 10:3-5

Ladies and gentlemen, we *have* to get involved in this fight—because if we leave it up to the world, there really is no hope. Just a lot more taxes to live in a much more violent place.

JUST BUILD MORE PRISONS

It breaks my heart that a growing number of voices today are crying out that the solution is found in more prison space. A 1991 study of hundreds of youths who passed through the Dade County, Florida, juvenile-justice system concluded that, despite seventeen million dollars spent on treatment programs, fully 90 percent became repeat offenders. That statistic prompted Anita Bock, a Dade County administrator, to lament, "It has now become utterly meaningless to be arrested. There is no effective rehabilitation."[4]

No effective rehabilitation—is that true?

Writer Eugene Methvin considered Ms. Bock's assessment and wrote, "In 1988, in a spasm of realism, the Florida legislature revised a sixty-one-year-old, largely unused 'habitual offender' law providing extended sentences for thrice-convicted criminals. That year, only 261 prisoners were serving 'habitualized' sentences. In just five years the number rose to 9,005. Slowing the revolving door in this way and keeping more repeaters behind bars helped Florida cut its crime rate 7.3 percent, though it remains the nation's highest. The locked-in habituals should number 17,000 by 1996—if the state builds the necessary prison space."[5]

What a solution! What a victory! Seventeen thousand people in Florida's jails! Now, I don't mean to suggest we should stop sending people to prison. We shouldn't and we can't. But is locking up people the best we can do?

The same writer a year later detailed several gruesome murders perpetrated by juveniles, then asked:

What can other states do to cope with the current wave of violent youth crime? They can start by taking three steps:

1. Record every arrest, fingerprint the offenders, and make juvenile records routinely available to adult courts. Otherwise, predators are treated as first offenders after the 18th birthday.

2. Impose graduated punishment for every offense. "Studies show repeatedly that punishment reduces both frequency and seriousness of offenses by young criminals and is most effective when it is consistently imposed for every offense," says University of Southern California psychologist Sarnoff Mednick. "These punishments don't have to be severe. But they have to be perceived as punishments."

3. Build the secure juvenile facilities we need. Americans should let their legislators, judges, and corrections officials know we expect them to keep violent offenders off the streets, whatever their age.[6]

Friends, the truth is, more kids are being locked up all the time. Youth are being remanded much more frequently to adult court. Typical of this trend is Multnomah County in Oregon. Late in 1991, the Multnomah County district attorney's office adopted a policy to remand young people who have criminal records and use guns to commit violent crimes. The policy also considers other aggravating factors, such as bias crimes and victims' injuries. "The numbers have increased and increased," Multnomah County District Attorney Michael D. Schrunk said of juvenile offenders. "It's because of what kids are exposed to—and what they're not exposed to—like street life and a lack of adult supervision."[7]

Again, I'm not against punishment or prisons. Unfortunately, they're both necessary. And sometimes it is for the benefit of society that a youth be treated like an adult.

But is this the best future we can come up with? Prisons in every county and jails on every corner? Is this the real hope of America? Thank God, it's not!

HOPE IN CHRIST

All across this country, Christians and concerned non-Christians are beginning to tackle the problem of youth violence in creative and effective ways. In faith they have launched out with new ideas, some of them radical, aimed at saving a few of our at-risk kids. They are making a real difference for good.

But we need so many more of them! Let me tell you about a few of the programs and organizations I know about which are reaching out to the hurting, bleeding young people of our nation. Maybe one of their stories will get your own creative juices flowing!

Boys Hope of Illinois is a nonprofit, privately funded organization which offers sixteen underprivileged boys, ages eleven to fourteen, a "ticket out of their poverty-stricken and crime-plagued neighborhoods" by providing them with housing in an affluent suburb and a full scholarship to either Loyola or St. Athanasius grammar schools in Evanston, Illinois.

Boys Hope provides these at-risk students with food, clothing, insurance, and a staff that serves as parents, cooks, tutors, counselors, and chaperones (the cost comes to about $30,000 a year per student). Strict house rules are enforced at Boys Hope: The boys must be well-groomed, tidy, studious, disciplined, and community-oriented. There is a 10 P.M. curfew with no excuses allowed.

Almost 90 percent of the boys who complete the program attend college. Some have graduated from prestigious schools such as Harvard University. About one in seven of the boys drop out of the program because they can't adjust to their new surroundings; the street has too strong a hold on them. The boys are allowed visits every other weekend with their families, and in the summer they have to find employment.

Boys Hope was established in 1977 by the Reverend Paul

Sheridan, a Jesuit priest from St. Louis. The program operates today in fourteen communities, and plans are being formulated right now to start a Girls Hope in 1995.[8]

I've already told you a bit about my "favorite church in the world," Victory Outreach of La Puente, California, pastored by my dear friend Sonny Arguinzoni. But, thank God, his is not the only congregation reaching out to the hurting youth of this country. Let me tell you about another compassionate church, founded by my own spiritual "father," David Wilkerson.

Times Square Church is a nondenominational Protestant church "of conservative evangelical doctrine and practice." It was founded in 1987 with a major emphasis on aid to the poor, the hungry, the destitute, and the addicted. (You'll remember that David founded Teen Challenge in 1959, a biblically-based program for the recovery of drug addicts. The federal government's own National Institute of Drug Abuse has certified it achieves a 70 percent cure rate. Teen Challenge currently operates 120 centers in the US and ninety overseas.)

Times Square Church holds six services weekly in a large opera-house-style theater—the Mark Hellinger on 51st and Broadway. Throughout the week it operates a multitude of ministries to reach out to the people who need it most.

The church's Upper Room Ministry is located in the troubled area of Eighth Avenue and West 41st Street and provides food and clothes to homosexuals and lesbians, people with AIDS, street people, the homeless, junkies, and alcoholics. It also organizes appropriate meetings for each of these groups.

Times Square's Hospitality Ministry finds jobs and housing for the homeless and unemployed. Its Prison Ministry conducts weekly Bible studies in three area correctional facilities, does regular one-on-one visitations and carries on letter correspondence. A special effort is made to evangelize inmates' immediate families as well as to help released inmates to reenter society. This ministry is staffed by 125 volunteers, including fifteen musicians and singers.

The church also operates Raven Mobile Food Truck, which goes every day into the poor neighborhoods of New York to provide food, warm clothing, and blankets. This is run by three hundred volunteers from Times Square Church!

Hannah House is an apartment house for women in need, including former addicts, alcoholics, and prostitutes. Its counterpart for men, Timothy House, aims to turn former addicts and alcoholics into men of God through solid Bible training, much prayer, and godly counseling.

I wish I had the time to tell you some of the remarkable stories that continue to come out of this ministry in the heart of America's largest city. Unfortunately, we don't have time. But I will tell you that, even today, at sixty-three years of age, David Wilkerson often goes out alone or with an assistant to walk through the streets near the church—along Broadway and Eighth Avenue and down "Crack Alley" on 41st Street. He's still looking for lost souls, just as he looked for me so many years ago. And he's still finding them.

What about you? What lost souls are you looking for? You don't have to go to New York or Times Square to find them. They're there, right under your nose, in your own city. Go find them! If God hasn't called you to a ministry like Victory Outreach or Times Square Church, there are still plenty of opportunities available.

God isn't limited by your gifting or your talents or your lack of experience. He's "limited" by only one thing: our lack of obedience. He can calm our fears—he really can! He can give us power— he really does! He can even give us a brand new vision—he really wants to! The only thing he can't do is obey for us.

That's our choice.

But enough conviction for now. Let me tell you about some other programs and tactics that people around the country are using successfully to combat the epidemic of youth crime and violence. Maybe you can use or adapt some of them in your own community.

A FEW IDEAS THAT WORK

Most experts agree that "guns and crack have become a deadly duo in inner cities," in the words of Bill Moyers.[9] Elizabeth Furse, a

Democratic US Congresswoman from Oregon, has said, "Police chiefs throughout the district have told me that they're often outgunned on the streets, and that assault weapons are among the most pernicious used during criminal acts. They added that these weapons serve no other purpose than to kill people."[10] So one of the places to start in this huge task is to reduce the number of guns on the streets. Alfred Blumstein of Carnegie Mellon University, formerly president of the American Society of Criminology, encourages us to "get guns out of the hands of the kids... Pursue the illegal gun market that is providing the guns to the kids. And shrink the drug market through a mixture of treatment of addicts, prevention, and diversion of addicts into other situations, such as the medical clinics established for heroin users."[11]

Moyers reports that a recent experimental program in Kansas City, Missouri, reduced crime in some areas by 50 percent after police started confiscating illegal guns.[12]

Stephen Teret of Johns Hopkins University has suggested that we treat guns like consumer products—childproof them or fit them with combination locks.[13] Don't laugh! The idea isn't so far out as it might seem.

The technology needed to detect guns invisibly is coming, an outgrowth of research done for US Navy nuclear submarines. Raytheon Company's sonar division is working on a civilian device that could be used in schools, banks, and convenience stores, or even by officers on the street.

"You could build the detectors into the walls," says a source with knowledge of the project. "You could walk by people while carrying a detector in your suitcase. You could drive by in a van. It would be totally nonobtrusive. People wouldn't even know they were being scanned."

The technological frisk is not the only high-tech crime fighter in the works. Alliant Techsystems of Minnesota, which also does sonar work for the Navy, has a project to place microphones on city telephone poles. At the sound of a gunshot, computers would triangulate the exact location and radio it to the police.

No need for a witness to dial 911. Police could be on the scene before perpetrators flee or before victims bleed to death.

David Boyd of the National Institute of Justice reports promising work on a "safe gun." With miniaturized recognition technology it could be fired only by its legal owner. Over the past twenty years, about one-fifth of police officers murdered by a firearm were shot with their own weapons or guns taken from fellow officers.

Thanks to Cold War research, a safer future is within our grasp.[14]

A number of organizations and projects are fighting back with programs that try to get members of the community involved. They all depend on networking resources, working together, and focusing on a few critical problems. (Hey—this sounds familiar. Isn't that what the church has been called to do?) Let me give you a sample of the "alphabet" groups I'm thinking of.

- **CRP: Community Reclamation Project.**
  The CRP aims to rid a community of gang activity through a series of programs designed to help unite community residents for one purpose: stamping out gangs. One of its underlying themes is to train neighborhood residents to combat gangs in the most efficient way possible. In some areas, CRP workers target areas with problems that are not so severe, but where people really want to get involved. That way, they can establish a good track record and show people in other parts of the city that gang prevention and control programs really do work. Program participants are taught to train other neighborhood residents; in that way, the CRP proliferates itself. The CRP's final aim is to stamp out gang activity in one neighborhood at a time so that eventually, all gang activity in the community will cease.[15]

- **BUILD: Broader Urban Involvement and Leadership Development.**
  BUILD is a nonprofit agency working with gang-involved youth

and "wannabes" to change negative behavior and improve their chances for a healthy, normal life. The program takes a threefold approach to rehabilitation: remediation, prevention, and community resource development.[16]

- **CIN: The Chicago Intervention Network.**
  CIN encourages local residents, law enforcement and social service workers to work together. A series of CIN storefront offices are located in low-income areas of the city. The organization seeks gang intervention through organizing extracurricular activities for young people, offering victim assistance programs, creating daily support programs to ensure at-risk youth have a positive home life, and encouraging neighborhood programs such as Neighborhood Watch and parent patrols. CIN operates a twenty-four-hour hotline which accesses a team of mobile social workers who specialize in immediate youth crises.[17]

- **APRC: The Arizona Prevention Resource Center.**
  This organization is similar to many across the United States. It is a cooperative effort of four state agencies (Governor's Office of Drug Policy; Arizona Department of Education; Arizona Department of Health Services; Arizona State University) and serves as a centralized source for individuals, schools, and communities to support, enhance, and initiate prevention efforts throughout Arizona. It is likely that a comparable group exists in your own state.[18]

- **GREAT: Gang Resistance Education and Training.**
  This federally funded program works to show kids they have alternatives to joining gangs or getting involved in other criminal activity. Children also learn they have to be responsible for their own actions. The program operates in public schools.[19]

WHAT YOU CAN DO NOW

The National Crime Prevention Council suggests there are four key things that every parent can do to help put gangs out of business:

1. Develop positive alternatives for your children (after-school and weekend activities, clubs, and sports; get older kids to mentor younger ones).

2. Talk with other parents. (Find out the straight scoop on what's happening with their kids, support each other, and thereby spot problems sooner.)

3. Work with police and other agencies. (Report suspicious activity, organize a Neighborhood Watch, tell police about gang graffiti, investigate other local services.)

4. Get organized against the gang organization. (Talk with your priest or minister, family counselor, community association, school counselor or principal, athletic coach; contact the Boys and Girls Club, YMCA and YWCA, Scouts; look for drug abuse prevention groups, youth-serving agencies, community centers.)[20]

It may help to know that young people associate with gangs on five general levels. Level 1: Fantasy (10 percent of gang affiliation); Level 2: At risk (20 percent); Level 3: Wannabe (40 percent); Level 4: Gang member (20 percent); Level 5: Veteran gangster (10 percent). Familiarity with such statistics can help to combat every child's complaint that "everybody's doing it!"[21]

Tony Ostos and Armando Raigosa, two experts who work with West Coast gangs, suggest the following steps:

- Discourage your children from hanging around with gang members.

- Occupy your children's free time.

- Develop good communication with your children.

- Spend time with your children.

- Do not buy or allow your children to dress in gang-style clothing.

- Set limits for your children.

- Do not allow your children to write or practice writing gang names, symbols, or other gang graffiti on their books, papers, clothes, walls, or any other place. Don't allow them to get gang tattoos.

- Develop an anti-gang environment in your household.

- Learn about gang and drug activity in your community.

- Participate in the education of your children.

- Participate in the community.

- Become an active parent, not a passive parent.[22]

Did you notice, once more, the emphasis on wholesome, healthy families? The best way to make sure your own kids don't get involved in the gangs is to make sure they know their real family loves and cares for them.

So let me ask you: Do your children know you love them? Without a doubt? *How* do they know it? These are questions none of us can afford to ignore.

HELP WITH SKIN ON IT

I've obviously reproduced just a sample of the kinds of ideas and programs already operating in America to stem the tide of youth violence. It would take volumes to catalog everything that's being tried. But one thing I know for sure: Nothing will ever take the place of human, skin to skin contact. Nothing!

Not even Jesus himself stayed at arm's distance from us wicked sinners when he came to save us. He didn't give advice or offer a suggestion or wish us luck. He didn't send money or a memo or a minion. He sent himself. He took on human "flesh and made his dwelling among us" (Jn 1:14). That is why he can completely "sympathize with our weaknesses"; he was "tempted in every way, just as we are—yet was without sin" (Heb 4:15).

Jesus is not only our Master—he is our model. We can follow in his footsteps and do what he did, because he now lives within us. He promised! In fact, his promise to us is even bigger than that!

I tell you the truth, anyone who has faith in me will do what I have been doing. He will do even greater things than these, because I am going to the Father.   **John 14:12**

Success Stories

I knew of a man in New York City who had a great job. When he got hooked on drugs, his wife kicked him out. He began to sleep under bridges and in the subways. One day he was passing Brooklyn Tabernacle Church, pastored by Jim Cymbala, a good friend of mine. He walked in smelling worse than a skunk hooked on Limburger cheese, but he talked to the pastor anyway. The pastor felt for him. In the beginning, his stench was overpoweringly repulsive, but this pastor saw (smelled?) beyond it. Here was a soul who needed help. This man wasn't begging for money any longer, but for Jesus; he was desperate for somebody to pray for him. The pastor took him in and this man was miraculously changed. Today he is a beautiful singer, he got his old job back, and he serves as one of the deacons in that church.

Remember, this pastor was dealing with a man who was literally kicked out of his own home. Only then did the man begin to understand how far he had fallen. Until the addict is faced, physically, with the consequences of his addiction, he won't change.

Just the other day I heard of a man named Oscar in Fresno, California. He was controlling his family through his drug addiction until he was given an ultimatum: face the problem or leave. He checked into a rehabilitation center, accepted Jesus, and was given the divine power to change. He made it! He is now a successful businessman.

Part of following in his footsteps is getting involved personally. We are to be "help with flesh on it." We could learn something from twenty-seven-year-old LaVon Van of Youth Outreach Youth Gangs, who acts as big brother to at-risk youth in Portland, Oregon. Van's agency operates under the umbrella of Portland's Northeast Coalition of Neighborhoods and was formed in 1988 in response to Portland's growing gang problem. Clients are referred by police, Portland public school officials, the courts, or through word of mouth.

"As a child, I was at risk," LaVon says. "I could have gone either way. Thank God people believed in me. That's what I want to do now—be the person who believes in these kids.... The kids think they know everything. I was the same way. I tell them that. I also say they can listen to my message now, or later they will wish they had listened to it.... I just want to tell these kids that they have potential. I want to show them that they can have nice things the positive way. They don't have to sell drugs or join a gang or shoot someone to make a name for themselves."[23]

I have no idea whether LaVon is a believer in Jesus Christ or not. But I do know he's doing something many of us aren't: He's following in Jesus' footsteps by reaching out to those who desperately need help.

How can we do any less?

MY TURN

I've given you a few ideas that others have tried in this nation-wide battle against youth violence. Now it's my turn! Let me offer a few of my own suggestions.

- I believe that in every inner city there's a "tower"—a man of God who is standing strong against the flood of evil and violence, a man who has already built a reputation for courage, insight, and service. More than anything else, these men need outside help in the form of prayer, people, and finances. I'm committed to finding these men wherever they are. I want to get in touch with them and put them on a computerized list as men worthy of support and needed resources. Maybe I'll call this the Inner-City Coalition. I'll let others tap into this resource to find out where the real warriors are both nationally and internationally. These men need our help, and I plan to give it to them. Do you know of such a tower? Then tell me about him. I want to come alongside and help.

- I want to encourage partnerships between suburban or rural churches and those in the inner city. This is already happening to a limited degree in some areas, but I want to encourage it to spread more widely. The precious resources of prayer, people, and finances shouldn't be hoarded. We need each other, and church partnerships can go a long way toward fleshing out Jesus' statement that the world will know we are his disciples if we love one another. Love takes action! Love works! I might even suggest a new song: "What the church needs now, is love, sweet love. It's the only thing that there's just too little of."

Suburban churches can become key players in supplying inner-city churches with spiritual ammunition: Bibles, Sunday school curricula, library resources, appropriate tapes, financial assistance for special projects. They can man the supply lines for some of God's frontline troops.

In my travels, I have come across a handful of suburban churches that actively support effective inner-city ministries. But to my disappointment, the majority have failed to back up the programs that daily risk the bullets, going face to face with violence, poverty, and drugs. We have *not* been like a mighty army, supplying the ministries on the front lines, giving them ammunition. We have not been there to help these people become the captains and generals on the front lines of the inner cities. We can't send them there with prayer alone; they need ammunition! We need to rise up with a great love for the gospel and for people. That is the great passion we must have.

- I'd like to suggest that appropriate churches set up shop in the neighborhoods where the kids are. Most of these kids wouldn't fit into a traditional church, and most church members wouldn't want to sit by a gang member or a drug addict. Yet the church must learn to mix like this, to become a place where "there is no Greek or Jew, circumcised or uncircumcised, barbarian, Scythian, slave or free, but Christ is all, and is in all" (Col 3:11).

- I'm calling for an invasion of retired teachers, professionals, and business people into the inner city. Teach these at-risk kids how to thrive. Show them that there's hope. Demonstrate that they can make it, then give them the training, skills, and resources they need to make it happen. You know, the Bible doesn't say anything about retirement. Moses never retired. Joshua never retired. Paul never retired. Peter never retired. You can look until your eyes pop, but you won't see the words "Palm Springs" anywhere in a concordance! Not "shuffleboard" or "all-day golfing" either. You retirees have a gold mine of experience and wisdom to offer. Don't waste it on tennis courts and Bermuda shorts. Our kids need you!

- I'd like to suggest that every Christian college in this nation open an inner-city clinic that brings in experts specializing in life skills or others working with gangs and related problems. You want your students to get an education? I guarantee this will open their eyes like they could never be opened sitting in a comfortable, air-conditioned, graffiti-free classroom. It might even do your professors some good—get them down out of those ivory towers for a while to see how badly they're leaning. Ivory towers don't stand for long when the castle's walls are blasted away! I already know of at least one college that's moving in this direction. Azusa Pacific University (Azusa, CA) is sending students to Victory Outreach to see how inner-city ministry works there. That's a good start, but it's only a start.

- I'm calling for property owners to give up inner-city property that they're not utilizing—whether that means church buildings, warehouses, abandoned stores, or whatever. There are worthy groups all over this country who are already at work in the inner city who lack the facilities and property they need to be effective. Hey, if you're not using it, and nobody's lined up at your door to buy it—why not give it away? It's biblical (see Acts 5, and remember not to shortchange the Lord!), it will help your brothers and sisters in the Lord, and it will please God. So go ahead, give it away. I promise, it won't hurt a bit.

THE BOTTOM LINE

We could go on listing possible ways to address the problem of youth violence from now until the new millennium—and those kinds of discussions can and must continue—but none of them will do a bit of good if we take our eyes off the bottom-line solution: Jesus Christ.

If we do not respond to the challenge the Lord is sounding today, we are going to wake up one of these days and see a wave of suicide and death. "Just Say No" is a joke. Why would a kid with chains of gold around his neck, diamond earrings, and five thousand dollars in his pocket say no to drugs? He needs something else. He needs something to fill the hole in his soul and give him hope.

He needs two kinds of love to make it—divine love and human love. There must be a mixture. For too long we have expected the Lord to change someone's life without our putting forth any effort.

The church of Jesus can no longer keep its eyes closed to the growing problem of our children. We are losing our youth, our future, to the gangs, to the needle, to crack, to cocaine, and to pornography. Did you know heroin is 23 percent stronger now than it was in the fifties and sixties?

You may not live in the inner city or next to a crack house. You may not hear the sound of gunfire every night as you go to bed. You may not have to wonder about your child walking to school through war zones, worrying if he or she will make it—or get shot in a drive-by shooting.

But even if you cannot imagine your child being attracted in any way to the gangs or to drugs, I assure you that he or she is still in danger. Our malls, parks, neighborhoods, and schools are all fertile recruiting grounds for the gangs. I know of pastors whose own children are involved in gang activity. I believe all of our lives will be touched very soon in one way or another by drugs, witchcraft, and the gangs. The gangs are becoming more sophisticated and organized. They are looking to the smaller towns, middle America, and the suburbs. It is a virgin market, ripe for the picking.

This is why we have to address the situation *now*. We have to reach the young kids in the large towns and the small. We have to give them a reason not to choose the gangs, drugs, or witchcraft. We have to give our youth a reason to believe in the family and the traditional, Bible-based beliefs that we follow.

Our kids need to see the love of Jesus... with skin on. That's you and me. If you're a believer, if you've got skin, you qualify.

Let's get busy!

CHAPTER 9

The Future Is in Our Hands

I t was the worst birthday I ever had. All around me swirled my family and my staff, those I love more than anyone in the world. I was surrounded by all the holiday trimmings that are supposed to make Christmas parties fun—delicious punch, fattening cookies and desserts of all kinds, festive holiday decorations, Christmas carols softly playing in the background. My own birthday was less than an hour away... and yet I was miserable, morose, and sullen. I was struggling to be cordial with the staff, and I could hardly get down the magnificent dinner which had been prepared for us.

The truth was, I couldn't stop thinking about Herman.

I had just returned from Huntsville, Texas, and a tour of the Ellis I Maximum Security Prison. I'd visited countless prisons before, and in my pre-Christian days I knew the inside of a cell as well as I knew the back of my hand. But this time, it was different.

I had been asked to come and minister to more than twelve hundred inmates at Ellis I in December 1994, as well as to speak to death row inmate Herman Clark. Herman, a convicted murderer, was scheduled to be executed by lethal injection just three days after my visit—on my birthday, December 6.

I had never been on death row before, and the experience unnerved me. Condemned men sat in their little cages a few feet from where I walked down the narrow hall to visit with Herman. When Herman first heard I was coming to visit, he requested that my host (Mike Barber, former wide receiver for the Houston Oilers, who leads an effective prison ministry at Ellis I) and I wait. It was a request born out of respect, not rudeness. Herman had been sitting in his little cubicle clothed only in his underwear, and he didn't want me to see him in that condition. So he asked if we could wait until he had the chance to put on some prison clothes.

When Mike and I finally took the long stroll past scores of men waiting for their turn at death—Texas is now executing death row inmates at the rate of one per day—I was shaken. I couldn't help but think that I myself had barely missed such a fate. I might easily have ended up in one of those cells, waiting for the executioner, just as Herman was.

Yet the man Mike and I spoke with on Saturday, December 3, was no longer a vicious, murdering thug. He had come to Christ while on death row, and he was now an example of how God can completely change a depraved, psychopathic animal into a humble, repentant man.

That's why I was so troubled at my staff's Christmas party. I knew Herman was scheduled to be executed at 12:08 A.M. Central Time—less than eight minutes away—and all I could think about was him.

I imagined the long, silent walk from his tiny cell to the place where the execution would take place—a cold, forbidding, antiseptic room outfitted with the tubes and needles and drugs that would pump quick death into Herman's veins. I thought of Herman's "last supper" just before midnight when he would enjoy communion with the other Christian men on death row. I imagined how they would take up the bread and the wine to remember the Lord's broken body and spilled blood—the Master's own death planned for and arranged by our Heavenly Father for our undeserving benefit. I saw in my mind's eye the earnest hugging and the hot tears and heard in my imagination the final good-byes that would have to be said.

Even though I had spent only a few, brief moments with Herman, I was certain he would go to his death singing of his Lord and Savior, Jesus Christ. And in fact, that's just what he did. The Huntsville paper reported the day after the execution that as the liquid was injected into his veins, Herman was singing softly and reading the Bible.

And so it happened that at 12:08 A.M., December 6—on the worst birthday of my life—Herman Clark slipped into unconsciousness, then death, then into the welcoming arms of Jesus.

A VOICE FROM THE GRAVE

My visit with Herman Clark on death row was one of the most painful things I've ever done—especially because I know we can prevent what happened to him in the lives of thousands of kids across the country. His end mirrors the future of far too many of our youth. His past is their future—unless we do something about it.

Herman's final words to us, captured on videotape, are like a voice from the grave. They remind me of Abel, who "by faith... still speaks, even though he is dead" (Heb 11:4). They remind me of Luke 16, where Jesus spoke of a young man in hell who pleaded with Abraham to send someone back to warn his brothers about their fate. Yet I know Herman's words are not a message from hell, but from heaven. He is now safely with Jesus, but he has left us with some vitally important words. I'd like you to drop in on our conversation.

Mike: Herman, how big is your home here?
Herman: Oh, roughly nine by six.
Mike: And this little area has been your home for how many years now?
Herman: Thirteen years.
Mike: For thirteen years. Monday, at midnight on December the sixth, unless you get a stay—and in your own words, you told me that's not likely...
Herman: Not likely.
Mike: ... you'll be going home to be with the Lord by lethal injection.
Herman: Amen!

Mike: How can you stand there in all honesty, with a smile from ear to ear, knowing that you're going to die in just a couple of days?

Herman: Because of the transforming, renewing power of Jesus Christ, through Almighty God's Holy Spirit. I mean, absolutely I know this.

Nicky: Then you're convinced of it.

Herman: Positively. I have no doubt about it. But let me say this. It hasn't always been a consistent walk with me, but I've known Jesus Christ and I know for a fact that God is a reality; he's not a myth. Prior to 1986 I didn't have any intimate knowledge of Christ. I didn't even know that his very presence could come from outside and come within me. But from the moment that I went down to the chapel on January 23, 1986, and accepted him publicly as my Lord and Savior and got baptized by immersion—all the way under the water—when I came up out of the water, I knew that there was a different presence within me. Until I started studying the Bible, I didn't know what it was. But once I started studying the Bible, I knew it was the Holy Spirit of God who came in.

This isn't a knowledge I had when I first came to death row. It's something that I learned since then. I'm not saying this to brag, but since 1986 I've read the Bible from Genesis to Revelation ten times, word for word, and I've read the New Testament twenty times. There's still a lot of spiritual understanding I need about Scripture, but as far as memory is concerned, nobody can tell me that, "well, this is in the Bible," because I have almost a perfect memory of what it says.

Scripture says Jesus Christ baptizes us into the Holy Spirit and the Holy Spirit baptizes us into Jesus Christ. So I know for a fact that the very presence of God came inside of me and I have no doubts about that.

There have been times when I haven't lived it and I felt like I wasn't worthy of it and maybe I lost it. But through another study of Scripture I realized that his love was absolute. Once he positionally makes us in Christ as Christ's righteousness, we can never lose that.

Nicky: Herman, there's something about you—that big smile, ear to ear—that has me wondering. On Monday, in two days, you're going to face death. And you're smiling. Are you ready?

Herman: Most definitely, because I know Jesus Christ as my Master and Kinsman Redeemer. Most definitely.

Mike: Herman, as you told me before the camera came on, in all likelihood you're not going to receive a stay of execution. In just a few days, you're going to die by lethal injection. Going through all of that—what does your heart say? What do you want to say to the people who are left behind, who maybe have loved ones going down that same, horrid trip, who are believing the lie of the devil? What would you say as a man who's been living for roughly thirteen years in a six-by-nine cell?

Nicky: You know, Mike, I believe that Herman has something to say. Right now, Herman, we have a heavy, serious problem with gangs and violence. Kids are killing kids. Parents are killing their children. I want you to send a message from your heart and leave a final statement. Tell the people what it means to be in the situation that you are in.

Herman: The main thing that I wish I had done as a child, as a teenager or a young adolescent, is to listen to my parents. On the average, the average child in America still has basically decent parents who have their best interests at heart.

The average gangs nowadays are made up of individuals who have no identity. Collectively they have an identity, but it's a wrong identity that's satanically inspired to bring hurt, hate, and anger into the world. The average person who joins a gang has to be "jumped in" by getting beat up, viciously, sometimes to the point of death. That's not true, pure love. That's hate. True, pure love does not hurt.

Joining the gang may give you some sense of belonging, it may give you some sense of companionship, but that's not what you really need. What you really need is somebody who loves you like your parents do, who tries to understand you, although it may not seem like they're listening to you all the time. They do love you. I absolutely know for a fact—I've seen it right here on death row—that many people get killed by being in gangs. It's not worth it, because if you die without knowledge of Christ, you're forever lost.

Nicky: Herman, I want you to send a message from your heart. If you could leave a last statement before you take the diploma that you are looking forward to from Jesus, what would it be? Do you really recommend to the teenagers that they should get to know Jesus? Do you really believe that Jesus would make a difference?

Herman: I absolutely know it! You see, the average teenager thinks that life is hopeless for them. But it's not! There's hope in Christ. I know that I'm forgiven. I know it without a doubt. My hope is in Christ. If you're trying to depend on humanistic reasoning and self-worth, it will never work. It's in Jesus Christ; it's about Jesus Christ. I absolutely know that.

I was once one of the most evil, corrupt-minded, perverted human beings who ever lived. But I know that in Christ, I'm seen by Almighty God as righteous in Christ. My hope is in Christ. It's not in some gang affiliation. I absolutely, positively know that.

Mike: Herman, in the last fifteen to twenty seconds we have together, what's the last thing you want to say?

Herman: I want to say that gangism is hurtful. It causes you to hurt other people like you don't want to be hurt. I saw a lady gangster on the Geraldo show one time named Angel, and it just made me cry and weep because she was raising her little child to be a gang member. Hurting people in the gangs is just not right because you yourself don't want to be hurt. Learn who the Lord Jesus Christ is and join his gangs. Join the holy gang of Almighty God!

Nicky: Praise the Lord!

Mike: Herman, would you want to say good-bye to your loved ones, to all your family? What would you say to them?

Herman: The whole world is my loved ones, and that's only because in Jesus Christ I love everybody enough to die for them. And because I love him like that I love you enough to die for you. If you were outside in a position of danger and I knew the Holy Spirit was leading me to jump in front of a car to save you, I could do that. I love the Lord like that because he loved us like that two thousand years ago when he got on a cross and died for us. I firmly believe that.

But specifically for my personal family, for those of you who knew me as a perverted, evil, corrupt person that I was: Since I've been on death row I've met Jesus Christ, and I want you to know I am a "Christ child." I am no longer the same person I was. I have changed and been transformed; I'm a new creature in Christ by the almighty power of my Daddy, who is God.

Nicky: Herman, when you take that walk in a couple of days, give this place a taste of glory. Go up there with dignity. Because the Lord is going to receive you with open arms. He's going to embrace you, kiss you. Your sins have been forgiven. You are a winner. And you're going to get your diploma. It's going to take a long time for me, but I'm going to get my diploma too. I'm going to graduate, I'm going to make it. I'm telling you, that's my goal.

Mike: Nicky, my friend told me this. If you are in Christ, we may meet for the first time, but never for the last time.

Nicky: That's right.

Mike: We'll see you again, Herman. And that's from the body of Christ.

OUR ONLY HOPE

Herman is with the Lord now, and although that comforts me, I still can't get the picture of his execution out of my mind. I'm troubled because so many of our precious youth are traveling down the same hopeless path that he followed.

Friends, it doesn't have to happen. We can close that pathway and barricade that road. But to do so we must take action now and bring the love of Jesus to the needy youth of America. Herman finally found Jesus' love, but it was too late. Too late for him, and too late for his victims.

The only hope for Herman and the youth of our cities is exactly the same hope that exists for us and which existed for God's ancient people, the Israelites. Do you know why the hope is the same for all of us? It's because our problem is the same: hearts that turn away from God, hearts that wallow in sin and wickedness, hearts that reject the good and choose the evil—in other words, hearts of stone.

When we call someone on the streets a "stone killer," we mean that they can murder someone in cold blood without a shred of conscience. But they're "stone killers" in another sense too. The reason they can do what they do is that their hearts are made of stone. They're cold. Lifeless. Dead. Their only hope is to receive a heart of flesh—and God is the only one who can provide it. As the Lord has told us:

I will give them an undivided heart and put a new spirit in them; I will remove from them their heart of stone and give them a heart of flesh.   **Ezekiel 11:19**

All through the centuries, this has been and remains our only hope. We will never be able to rehabilitate hearts of stone. We can never in a million years reform hearts of stone. We will never succeed in retraining them, improving them, revitalizing them, or reviving them. Why not? Because stone is dead. Lifeless. Cold. Hard.

But a heart of flesh—ah, that's a different story! A heart of flesh can be moved with great compassion toward the very people a heart of stone can kill and rape and maim. People whose hearts of stone have been replaced with hearts of flesh can joyfully relate to God, to each other, and to the rest of God's creation.

But how does a person get this heart of flesh? How does he or she get rid of a heart of stone? The Bible gives a single answer in several ways.

The writer of Hebrews encourages us to "draw near to God with a sincere heart *in full assurance of faith*, having our hearts sprinkled to cleanse us from a guilty conscience" (Heb 10:22, emphasis added).

The apostle Peter, speaking at the first church council, said, "Brothers, you know that some time ago God made a choice among you that the Gentiles might *hear from my lips the message of the gospel and believe.* God, who knows the heart, showed that he accepted them by giving the Holy Spirit to them, just as he did to us. He made no distinction between us and them, for he *purified their hearts by faith*" (Acts 15:7b-9, emphasis added).

And the apostle Paul wrote, "The god of this age has blinded the minds of unbelievers, so that they cannot see the light of the gospel of the glory of Christ, who is the image of God. For we do not preach ourselves, but Jesus Christ as Lord, and ourselves as your servants for Jesus' sake. For God, who said, 'Let light shine out of darkness,' *made his light shine in our hearts* to give us the light of the knowledge of the glory of God in the face of Christ" (2 Cor 4:4-6, emphasis added).

A living faith in the Lord Jesus Christ, who died on the cross for our sins and was raised to life on the third day, is the rock-solid basis of our hope.

As I've said throughout this book, the *only* hope for our cities and our nation is a genuine revival in which men and women, boys and girls from the inner cities, from the suburbs, and from rural communities repent of their sin and turn their lives over to Jesus Christ.

Jesus Christ is the only hope for young gangsters.
Jesus Christ is the only hope for old gangsters.
Jesus Christ is the only hope for hardened, inner-city youth.
Jesus Christ is the only hope for hardened, suburban grandmas and grandpas.
Jesus Christ is the only hope for blacks.
Jesus Christ is the only hope for Hispanics.
Jesus Christ is the only hope for Asians.
Jesus Christ is the only hope for whites.
Jesus Christ is the only hope... *for you!*

For almost two hundred pages now I've been talking about the violence that's spreading across this nation through the gangs and other angry youth. It's easy to look in the cold, dead eyes of a young eleven-year-old killer and proclaim that he needs Christ to replace his heart of stone with a heart of flesh. But we can't stop there! Without Christ, any one of us could become a stone killer, because all of us are born with hearts of stone!

There is no one righteous, not even one;
there is no one who understands,
no one who seeks God.
All have turned away,
they have together become worthless;
there is no one who does good,
not even one.
Their throats are open graves;
their tongues practice deceit.
The poison of vipers is on their lips.
Their mouths are full of cursing and bitterness.
Their feet are swift to shed blood;
ruin and misery mark their ways,
and the way of peace they do not know.
There is no fear of God before their eyes.　　　Romans 3:10-18

I am an evangelist who's nearing the end of his book, and so I have to ask you: What about your own heart? I am so grateful that you are committed to the youth of this nation, that you have taken a good chunk of your time to read this book. I am glad that you care enough to want to do something about America's youth emergency. But I have to ask you: What about your own heart? Where do you stand with Jesus Christ?

It was the apostle Paul who told us, "If you confess with your mouth, 'Jesus is Lord,' and *believe in your heart* that God raised him from the dead, you will be saved. For it is *with your heart that you believe* and are justified, and it is with your mouth that you confess and are saved. As the Scripture says, 'Anyone who trusts in him will never be put to shame'... for 'Everyone who calls on the name of the Lord will be saved'" (Rom 10:9-11,13, emphasis added).

If you have already put your trust in Jesus, I want to say "Hallelujah!" But if you haven't yet come to the place where you have asked him to take out your heart of stone and replace it with a heart of flesh, I want to invite you to do that right now. The best place for you to start addressing the desperate needs of America's hurting youth is by getting a new heart of your own. All you have to do is ask, in your own words.

Once you're fully on Jesus' team—not just in the cheering section, but in uniform and on the field—then together we can begin to make a difference in the lives of the forgotten people of the inner cities of America.

MAKING A DIFFERENCE

And what are we to do about these forgotten people? What can be done? Who will seek them out—to touch them and care for them?

Does God care about them?

Yes, he certainly does! He deeply cares, enough to put his very heart inside hundreds and now thousands of people and cause them to feel the raw and unquenchable pain that he feels and to know the consuming urgency to hurry, to go, to care, to reach out, and to see those needs met.

I believe a great army is being raised up. And you know what? You can be part of it, my friend.

I am running across more and more young men and women who have totally committed their lives to the Lord, some in their early teens. Many of them have an obvious anointing. They remind me of Paul and how he had a Timothy, someone in whom he saw a fire and whom he could teach and train to lead the next generation. Most importantly, these kids have a respect and fear for the Lord. His hand is noticeably on them.

I take these young people very seriously. It's such an encouragement to me, because I know they will inherit my experience and knowledge and will run with the torch long after I am gone. They are part of the army that the Lord is raising up in these days.

But this is no easy mission. Heeding the call to reach out to the rejects of our increasingly selfish and self-centered society is difficult and even dangerous. Yes, God will protect and guide you. He will never leave you alone. He will not call everyone to the same battle fronts—but he does call all of us to the war.

And there are such rewards! How often I hear people say that they wish they could "see God." They long to feel his presence here in this fallen world. They tell me, "If only I could see his face, hear his voice, feel him near."

I wonder how often the Lord says to us, "Here I am—in this hurting man, in this lonely woman, in this abandoned child. Here I am! In the ghetto. In the barrio. In the projects. On the streets. Here I am! Here I am! Come and touch me!"

What if all the Christians in the world... or just in America... or just in California... or just in one little town... or just in one little church... or just in one family... got to work?

We would see a revolution—just like we are beginning to see around the world. We would see people snatched away from death and despair and given new life!

REVIVAL IN UNLIKELY PLACES

Sometimes we are so close to the forest that we can't see the trees. If you're tempted to think that the grave problems of America's inner cities are unsolvable and beyond hope, I think you need to take a step back. You've got bark in your eyebrows and sap in your eyes.

The truth is, God does his best work in unlikely places. He loves to reach down to "impossible" situations and touch them with his power, transforming them by his grace into shining examples of his handiwork. I'd like to step back with you for a moment from America's youth emergency to tell you about another place and another crisis. Perhaps by seeing the great hope that God is bringing to that place, you will begin to believe that there is also great hope for America's inner cities.

But before I take you there, let me ask you to be on the lookout for the many similarities between these two crises. In both, God's people are learning that prayer accomplishes much. In both, believers are remembering that God has his own timetable and that he acts in his own time—but he does act! In both, the children of God are learning that no situation is beyond hope or too far gone for God to triumph. In both, Christians are rediscovering the power of forgiveness. In both, churches are beginning to see that working cooperatively can pull off miracles, even where organized criminal activity and racial tension are ever-present threats. And in both, God's people are learning that opposition can take many forms, but the response is always the same: commitment in prayer and absolute reliance on the power of the Holy Spirit.

Now you're ready to take a trip with me. We'll be visiting a country where more than five thousand mafioso are menacing the population. They were under wraps until recently, but now all hell is breaking loose. These are trained killers, formerly with the state's secret police—the KGB. I want to take you to the former Soviet Union.

In October 1994, we held our first ever crusades in Tallinn, Estonia, and in St. Petersburg, Russia. Over the years I had received requests to come to Russia but it was not until this trip that I felt the time was right to go. We had been planning this trip for nearly a year. While I was ministering in Virginia, my daughter, Alicia, and son-in-law, Patrick, went over a few days early to make sure of last-minute details. It turned out to be very important that they went over early. We realized that we were going to new territory, but we had no idea the extent of the opposition that we would encounter. The following is a fax that I received from them before I left the USA:

Greetings from Estonia!

After flying in, we have been in meetings all day with the Christians here and something urgent has come up. The enemy is trying to distract and discredit the crusades through the media. Here are two examples we will share with you so that you can tell others to pray:

1. They have advertised the crusade as "Come hear ex-gang leader from New York, not a preacher, at Tallinn City Hall." The largest and most widely read newspaper in Estonia featured an ad saying, "Come hear former preach-er from New York, now a gang leader, at [some local bar]." The ad is large and depicts a Latin man with a woman. Both are naked in a bathtub. The picture is *very explicit!*

2. A renowned Russian astrologer publicly predicted the recent sinking of the ferry off the coast of Estonia that tragically took over nine hundred lives. This prediction was published two days before the disaster occurred. This same astrologer, who is trusted by many, is now saying a great evil will be unleashed. The evil he described is one of "rape and cannibalism," so he has urged people to stay in, especially women. According to him, this great evil is starting on Thursday, which coincidentally is the first night of the Russian-speaking crusade in Estonia, and then continuing throughout the rest of the crusade evenings.

3. We just heard tonight that the Russian Orthodox church is strongly opposing the crusades in St. Petersburg and denouncing them as evil. They have pledged to send one thousand Orthodox pastors to disrupt the meetings.

... We expect great things to happen in the next couple of days, nevertheless we need much prayer. Please contact the following and ask them to intercede for these concerns. Pray the "strongman" that is over Estonia will be bound and that the Gospel will be free to liberate these captive souls....

-Alicia and Patrick

I instructed my office to send this fax to my home church, the Victory Outreach churches, and David Wilkerson's church in Times Square, to name a few. The prayers that were lifted to heaven were the reason the attacks did not hinder the crusades. Gloria and I felt those prayers carried us through the next five eventful days.

We arrived in Tallinn on the day of the first crusade. A week before my arrival, the ferry mentioned earlier sank off the coast of Tallinn, resulting in the loss of more than nine hundred lives. This national disaster had riveted the attention of the country on the innocent lives who had been enveloped by the freezing Baltic Sea, and soberly focused the nation on the uncertainty of life. The entire country of Estonia was in mourning.

Yet the Lord did some amazing things even in the midst of the disaster. We discovered that a group of thirty Swedish youth had come over to Estonia to help prepare for our crusade. Before they got on the boat to return home, one girl had a dream that the ferry would sink. No one believed her. Then a short while later another girl had a similar dream. Suddenly this group of Swedish Christians became convinced that they had received marching orders from God to evangelize the boat before it went down. After this second warning, they felt as if they were supposed to be on the ferry.

As soon as they got aboard for the trip home, they began to witness to anyone who would listen. This handful of Swedish kids began singing and leading people to Christ. Soon the water grew choppy and the ferry's electricity went out. The kids ran up to people and told them to call out to Jesus, that he could save them. Even as the ship started to sink, some of the kids stayed down on the lower decks to witness to the elderly people who were consigned below deck. Kids led men and women to Christ even as the ferry was slipping beneath the cold, cold waves. They willingly gave up their lives to bring others into the kingdom. Only one of the group's members decided to stay behind, and only two members survived the sinking to tell about what had transpired on board.

Just as we arrived in Estonia, the government was in the process of approaching local churches to provide counseling about the sinking. After we arrived, the Christians involved in the crusade watched expectantly, wondering what message I could bring to their people, and the Lord did give me one.

The first evening I preached in the Tallinn city hall and the message was translated into Estonian. In preparation for this, the movie *The Cross and the Switchblade* had been shown on national TV the night before. Local Christians told me this was the first time ever the city hall attracted a full crowd for a Christian event. We were so excited to hear that some people had prophesied years before that Christians would one day be preaching the gospel in the biggest halls in Estonia. *They felt that our crusades were the answers to these prophecies and that they had never seen so many churches united and working together.*

In 1991, Estonia became the first republic to gain its independence after being ruled by Russia since 1721. There is still a strong Russian presence in Estonia. Many former KGB members are now involved with the Mafia. There are deep-rooted feelings of hatred between the Estonians and the Russians. My message was a simple one of forgiveness. If the Estonians were to go anywhere as a nation, they not only had to accept the forgiveness of Christ, they also had to forgive their former oppressors. The altar was filled with hundreds who were reaching out to Christ.

One of the local sponsors and a humble man of great faith, Peter Vosu, had been held captive five years earlier by the KGB for his Christian beliefs. His possessions were taken away from him and he was told that if he did not reveal where he was receiving his Christian literature, he would never see his family again and his children would be put in a state-run orphanage. Now he is free to share his faith. He reminds me of Paul's words, "I am suffering even to the point of being chained like a criminal. But God's word is not chained" (2 Tm 2:9).

Peter had a friend who was a criminal and who had spent time in prison. A week before the crusades, this man gave his heart to the Lord. That man was at the crusade and told Peter that he saw several "big Mafia bosses coming forward for prayer!"

I addressed forgiveness again the second night, which was aimed at the Russians who were now living in Estonia. Because of my background as an abused child and my parents' involvement in the occult, I was able to relate my struggles with forgiveness. The response of the people was fantastic. It was no coincidence that many hearts had been softened by the recent ferry tragedy. The people were ripe and ready to hear this powerful message of the gospel.

We worked closely with a mission group from Finland in planning for the crusades. The Finns have been actively smuggling Bibles and working with the underground church in Estonia for years. I was told that the book *The Cross and the Switchblade* had been translated into Estonian. Five handwritten copies of the book had been passed around the country for years! My translator, Ulo Niinemagi, was one of the men who had distributed the handwritten book. He belonged to the oldest church in Estonia, Oleviste Church, which had been built in 1267. From the spire of this church the KGB used to broadcast their communist propaganda throughout the Soviet occupation. But since 1991, a Christian radio station has replaced the former KGB station and now broadcasts Christian music and sermons!

ON TO ST. PETERSBURG, RUSSIA

We flew into St. Petersburg on the third day of the trip. St. Petersburg is a sprawling city of five million. It was founded and built by Peter the Great and was the former capital of Russia.

Immediately before we arrived, the ruble had dropped in value 30 percent and the people had gone into survival mode. Girls openly sold their bodies, lining up in St. Petersburg's second best hotel. Take your pick: blonde, redhead, brunette, whatever you desired. The Mormons have moved into the country, as have other cults and devotees of the New Age. Witchcraft is strong. Many Russians have walked away from the true faith because the only Christianity they have seen is a television version of American churchianity, and they think it's a show, pure Hollywood. Shortly before our visit, an American television ministry tried to import American cultural ways and the audience walked out of the hall.

Russians don't need to hear about prosperity, they need to hear how to forgive a father who raped them or an uncle who betrayed them. Our translator during the crusades was an elegant lady who previously had served as the translator for Elizabeth Taylor. When I began to describe my family background, this polished lady broke down and had to leave the stage. We discovered immediately that this is a land of deep hurts and long-term pains.

We had left the land of milk and honey and had arrived at a place that profoundly touched all of us. These people had lived in a cage, and now they were experiencing freedom for the first time.

I insisted on visiting an "underground" church while we were there. Laughter had deserted that congregation long ago, but as I began speaking to them and sharing my testimony, a few smiles cracked here and there and a few people actually chuckled.

The pastor of the church represented third-generation leadership. His grandfather spent two decades in prison; eventually the authorities let him out to die. His son took over and quickly followed his dad's footsteps into prison. Now the grandson was in charge—a young man of about twenty-eight. Every night for two years Dmitri had stood on the steps of the Museum of Atheism and preached to whomever would listen. He began this practice immediately before communism fell, and now has built the church to a regular attendance of about two thousand. City officials have given his church a coliseum that will seat five thousand, with the understanding that the church will help the poor, take care of the elderly, and otherwise relieve the government of burdensome human responsibilities.

Dmitri has worn the same shoes, socks, pants, and coat every evening for the past several years. I had the privilege of giving him my own suit. It wasn't much of a gift—used suits, after all, can be found in any Goodwill across this affluent nation—but he was moved to tears by the present.

Needs are everywhere in Russia. There are somewhere between ten and twenty thousand orphans in St. Petersburg alone. The orphanages are run by the Orthodox church, which wouldn't let us visit these lonely kids. In the past, the state would remove kids from the homes of "enemies of the state," which often meant Christians. A lot of Western people want to adopt these children, but the church won't let them.

Yet what really moved me the most as an evangelist during our trip were the two hundred or so kids from Finland who came to Russia to help publicize our crusades. They were full of God, burning with desire to witness for Jesus. They took the city by storm and would witness to anyone, despite frequent (and even violent) opposition. They were excited and on fire in a way I haven't seen in the United States for many years. They won people to Jesus like nobody's business—and they were only two hundred kids. Can you imagine what would happen if we turned loose one million on-fire kids in America? We'd crack the crackers!

The Christians in St. Petersburg had been promoting the crusades all summer, handing out some five hundred thousand flyers. Our services were held on three successive evenings in Lenin Hall, the largest auditorium in Europe. Each evening hundreds and hundreds came to the altar to give their lives to Christ! My autobiography, *Run, Baby, Run*, was translated into Russian and ten thousand copies arrived fresh off the press for the last evening of the crusade. We handed out these copies at no charge to the people. We also wrote an illustrated evangelistic booklet for children.

While there I also had the privilege of meeting with sixty of the local pastors and their wives. I stressed to them the importance of unity. We had been told that because of interchurch strife, *most of the pastors had never been in the same room together.*

I noticed the youth of the country were confused, distrustful, and angry. Many are ready to revolt again. Yet some have already found their answers in Christ—and are paying for it. Four young Russian boys who were handing out tracts inviting people to the evening services were beaten up and sent to the hospital. Three of them tried to make it back to the crusades the next day, but two of them were forced to return to the hospital afterward. Their injuries were that serious. Yet they didn't harbor any resentment toward those who beat them up. One young man whom we captured on film said he felt honored to be beaten up for the Lord.

One day we were driving down the Nevsky Prospekt in St. Petersburg and saw a commotion on the city square. We noticed two groups. On one corner, two hundred Finnish and Russian youth were promoting the evening crusade. They were holding up banners and signs, singing praise and worship choruses while different individuals took the microphone and shared their personal stories. In another part of the square a pro-communist demonstration was in full swing, complete with red communist flags, pictures of Stalin, songs about the glory of the old days, and posters describing the United States as "Satan's nest." When the Christian youth were witnessing for Jesus, they were approached by older people, in their sixties and seventies, who violently protested the gospel that was being proclaimed in the streets. On this city square, you could see starkly portrayed the struggle going on for the very soul of this nation and people.

St. Petersburg, and Russia for that matter, has a long way to go. There is no guarantee that they will continue to enjoy political freedom. The people are having a hard time just being able to buy necessities, like their daily food. Yet my sincere hope is that Russia will make it through this turbulent period. If communism should ever return and Christian ministries be kept out of the country, I believe that God has allowed us to play an important part in helping the Christians evangelize their own people. But whether or not the former Soviet countries become closed again to outside influences, we witnessed the message of Jesus Christ *breaking the chains and bringing freedom to many hearts!* We saw firsthand what Jesus meant when he said, "You will know the truth, and the truth will set you free" (Jn 8:32). Several of the Mafia ringleaders in St. Petersburg came forward during our crusade to ask Christ into their lives!

I am thankful that the Lord has allowed my life to be used in reaching the people of Russia. I had been asked to go to Russia on many occasions in the past. For one reason or another, a trip was never accomplished. After this trip I finally understood why he had ordained the trip for this specific time. The problems the Russians are facing are new to them, but they aren't new to me. With freedom also came tremendous problems with crime. I was not in the country even twelve hours when my wife and I observed drugs, prostitution, and the Mafia around our hotel! The church there has a very naive and passive outlook on crime, seeing it as something they can't have an effect upon.

I began to see that God's timing was perfect, as always. It took a few years for these problems to develop and now they are blatantly evident on the streets. Because of my experience in dealing with drug addicts and criminals, I know that these problems grow and spread like cancer and only worsen. They can destroy a country. I would love to return someday and help the Christians see that they play a key part in evangelizing the outcasts who seem unreachable.

THE FUTURE IS OURS

Do you see why I have such hope for the inner cities of America and for the hurting youth of this country? We serve a God with whom nothing is impossible. The darker the situation, the brighter he shines! Just a few months before we left for Estonia, no one thought the Iron Curtain would ever fall. But it did—with a crash!

In the same way, there are some who believe gang violence in this country has gone too far to be turned around. They see the sky-rocketing statistics of youth crime and shake their heads, declaring that nothing can be done. It's too late, they say.

They're wrong.

If we seek God, if we search our own souls, if we band together for one purpose, we *will* find a remedy. The part we play in finding the solution will be different for each of us. But each of us will have a part. We need to enlarge our hearts so that our concern for kids does not stop at our backyard fence. We need to restore the sense of community, where neighbor can call on neighbor, where troubled kids can find a second home, even if it's just the one next door.

If the church really does become a Holy Ghost Hospital, then revival will begin in the inner city. God will show his power and his might by transforming the very part of culture that many think is irredeemable.

I believe we stand at the threshold of a coming, earth-shaking revival. I believe God is about to act in such an astonishing way in the inner cities of the world that the rest of humanity will have to sit up and take notice. I believe that the prophecy of Acts 2:17-21 is about to take place, starting in the inner cities:

In the last days, God says,
I will pour out my Spirit on all people.
Your sons and daughters will prophesy,
your young men will see visions,
your old men will dream dreams.
Even on my servants, both men and women,
I will pour out my Spirit in those days,
and they will prophesy.
I will show wonders in the heaven above
and signs on the earth below,
blood and fire and billows of smoke.
The sun will be turned to darkness
and the moon to blood
before the coming of the great and
glorious day of the Lord.
And everyone who calls on the name of the Lord
will be saved.

And I'm not alone! A few years ago David McKenna, president of Asbury Theological Seminary, wrote a book called *The Coming Great Awakening*. In his introduction he said this:

I am a realistic optimist. Simply put, I do not believe that God has given up on our world.... When we glance quickly at the decades since World War II, we can see the signs of the Lord preparing us for another Great Awakening.... God raises up visionary leaders with prophetic voices just as he promised in his Word. The American church awaits the vision and voice of prophetic leaders who will show the way through the moral jungle of our time; the church awaits the outpouring of God's Spirit in the final decade of the twentieth century. The culture also groans for deliverance from the forces of decay which threaten our future. Only a Great Awakening can make the difference in rebuilding the moral base on which our freedom rests. Revival among the masses, renewal in the church and reform in the culture is the full cycle of a Great Awakening.

Is another Great Awakening on the way as we come to the close of the twentieth century? The answer is yes. We have the *pattern* of American history, the *perspective* of global revival, and the *promise* of God's Word.... We can foresee another Great Awakening. For now, we must watch and wait; watch the stirring of God's Spirit and wait for the outpouring when the young see visions. In those visions we see our hope.[1]

But could this really happen? Could a great revival actually sweep our nation to such an extent that crime would be slashed and our streets would become safe once more?

It has happened before; why not again? When the first Great Awakening thundered across England in the 1700s, people actually once followed John Wesley home after he had given a sermon and said to him, "Tell us more." Wesley then spoke for another hour by candlelight and the people crowded around his home, thirsty for the message of the Lord. Many historians credit the move of God sparked by Wesley for saving England from the kind of bloody revolution that tore apart France.

The Second Great Awakening took place a century or so later and reshaped the spiritual landscape of America. Charles Finney was used by God to reach hundreds of thousands for Christ. D.L. Moody followed Finney and spread the revival to England.

At the beginning of our own century, another mighty revival spread from shore to shore. In cities between Iowa and Colorado, twelve hundred people gathered for prayer meetings in city halls. Stores were closed on Sundays and corrupt officials were voted out of office. Across the ocean in Wales, one hundred thousand people were converted, drunkenness was cut in half, and crime was so diminished that police became unemployed in some districts. And the wave of revival spread from there to Korea, India, and Latin America.

Yes, there *is* great hope for us! There is hope for our youth, hope for our cities, hope for our nation and our world. You see, it is not where you start, but where you finish. We're in a race.

In the midst of the race, it's crucial that we don't lose heart. Oh, sure, we're bombarded by temptations, hardships, and disappointments. We get our hearts broken time and again. We've gone through all of that.

We must remember that not only did Jesus save us, but he keeps us. We are not left alone in this race. We do not fight this battle by ourselves. The Lord didn't send us out alone to fight the forces of darkness. He is the kind of General who leads his troops into the fire fight, striding irresistibly forward at the head of his holy army.

Even when it looks like the devil's forces are winning, God can take those very circumstances and turn them around to his glory. A little church in Oriente, Cuba, illustrates my point.

For years this church had asked Castro's communist government for permission to renovate its dilapidated facilities. Each year the government refused. Then one year, the state reversed itself and gave approval. Church members joyfully tore off the roof and started knocking down the walls, only to have the government reverse itself once more and deny permission to rebuild. It certainly seemed as if Satan had won a great victory.

But God wasn't done!

Wrote Herbert Schlossberg, "The Lord has used the situation in an interesting way. Since the building has no walls the preaching and hymns are heard in the neighborhood much more clearly than if the church had been enclosed. More people are hearing the gospel this way."[2]

God took a "clear" defeat and turned it into a major victory! And he can do it for us as well.

Friends, we can win this war. God invites each of us to take our place in the ranks. The battle is his; we are simply asked to join him.

Businesses have 800-numbers for anyone who wants to call free of charge. I think churches should have 800-numbers for those who need help. For emergencies we have 911; churches should have "Call Psalm 91:1—He who dwells in the shelter of the Most High will rest in the shadow of the Almighty." Or they might try Psalm 50:15—"Call upon me in the day of trouble; I will deliver you, and you will honor me."

It is the church's task to help make those verses come alive. They are "emergency" verses, and they are especially appropriate for a culture living under the threat of a Code Blue.

In the great revival that I believe is coming to this nation, starting in its inner cities, I extend to you an invitation to enlist in the Lord's army—especially if you're a medic. The youth emergency is real and the casualties are mounting. But I believe with all my heart that by working together and being guided and empowered by his Spirit, we can turn this Code Blue emergency into a white hot celebration for Jesus.

The Root of Our Problem

I read a fascinating article recently based on a speech delivered by William Bennett, the former US "drug czar" in the Bush administration. Bennett was speaking at The Heritage Foundation in Washington, D.C., and offered an unusual analysis of this country's woes. That is, his ideas don't get much of a hearing in our nation's capital these days. But he's right on target! What he had to say that day was so good and so appropriate for what we're talking about in this chapter that I'd like to reproduce nearly all the article.[1] See if you don't agree with Bennett's diagnosis of our country's root problem:

A few months ago I lunched with a friend who now lives in Asia. During our conversation the topic turned to America as seen through the eyes of foreigners. My friend had observed that while the world still regards the United States as the leading economic and military power on earth, this same world no longer beholds us with the moral respect it once did, as a "shining city on a hill." Instead, it sees a society in decline.

Recently, a Washington, D.C., cabdriver—a graduate student from Africa—told me that when he receives his degree, he is returning to his homeland. His reason? He doesn't want his children to grow up in a country where his daughter will be an "easy target" for young men and where his son might also be a target for violence at the hands of other young males. "It is more civilized where I come from," he said.

Last year an article in *The Washington Post* described how exchange students adopt the lifestyle of American teens. Paulina, a Polish high school student studying in the United States, said that when she first came here she was amazed at the way teenagers spent their time. "In Warsaw, we would come home after school, eat with our parents, and then do four or five hours of homework. Now, I go to Pizza Hut and watch TV and do less work in school. I can tell it is not a good thing to get used to."

I have an instinctive aversion to foreigners harshly judging my nation; yet, I must concede that much of what they say is true. Something has gone wrong with us.

Yes, there are families, schools, churches, and neighborhoods that work. But there is a lot less virtue than there ought to be.

Last year I compiled *The Index of Leading Cultural Indicators*, a statistical portrait of American behavioral trends of the past three decades. Among the findings: Since 1960, while the gross domestic product has nearly tripled, violent crime has increased at least 560 percent. Divorces have more than doubled. The percentage of children in single-parent homes has tripled. And by the end of the decade 40 percent of all American births and 80 percent of minority births will occur out of wedlock.

These are not good things to get used to.

The United States leads the industrialized world in murder, rape and violent crime. At the same time, our elementary school students rank at or near the bottom in tests of math and science skills. Since 1960, average SAT scores in our high schools have dropped seventy-five points.

In 1940, teachers identified the top problems in America's schools as: talking out of turn, chewing gum, making noise, and running in the hall. In 1990, teachers listed drugs, alcohol, pregnancy, suicide, rape, and assault.

These are not good things to get used to, either.

There is a coarseness, a callousness, and a cynicism to our era. The worst of it has to do with our children. Our culture seems almost dedicated to the corruption of the young.

Last year, Snoop Doggy Dogg, indicted for murder, saw his rap album "Doggystyle," which celebrates marijuana use and the degradation of women, debut at No. 1 on the pop chart. What will happen when young boys who grow up on mean streets, without fathers in their lives, are constantly exposed to such music?

On television, indecent exposure is celebrated by all ages as a virtue. There was a time when personal failures, subliminal desires and perverse tastes were accompanied by guilt, or at least silence. Today they are tickets to appear as guests on talk shows. In one recent two-week period, these shows featured cross-dressing couples, a three-way love affair, a man who fools women into thinking he is using a condom during sex, and prostitutes who love their jobs. These shows present a two-edged problem: people want to expose themselves, and other people want to watch.

We have become inured to the cultural rot that is setting in. People are losing their capacity for shock, disgust and outrage. During the 1992 Los Angeles riots, Damian Williams was filmed crushing an innocent man's skull with a brick, while Henry Watson held the victim down. When Williams was finished, he did a victory dance. Watson and Williams' lawyers then built a legal defense on the premise that people cannot be held accountable for getting caught up in mob violence. ("I guess maybe they were in the wrong place at the wrong time," one juror told *The New York Times.*) When these men were acquitted on most counts, the sound you heard throughout the land was not outrage, but relief.

This is not a good thing to get used to.

What's to blame for this change? The hard fact is that it was not something done to us; it is something we have done to ourselves. Thoughtful people have pointed to materialism, an overly permissive society, or the legacy of the 1960s. There is truth in almost all these accounts. But in my view our real crisis is spiritual, a corruption of the heart.

The ancients called our problem acedia, an aversion to spiritual things and an undue concern for the external and the worldly. Acedia also is the seventh capital sin—sloth—but it does not mean mere laziness. The slothful heart is steeped in the worldly and carnal, hates the spiritual and wants to be free of its demands.

When the novelist Walker Percy was asked what concerned him most about America's future, he answered, "Probably the fear of seeing America, with all its great strength and beauty and freedom... gradually subside into decay through default and be defeated, not by the communist movement, but from within, from weariness, boredom, cynicism, greed, and in the end helplessness before its great problems."

I realize this is a tough indictment. If my diagnosis is wrong, then why, amid our economic prosperity and military security, do almost 70 percent of the public say we are off track? I submit that only when we turn to the right things—enduring, noble, spiritual things—will life get better.

During the last decade of the twentieth century, there is a disturbing reluctance to talk seriously about matters spiritual and religious. We have become used to not talking about the things that matter most. One will often hear that religious faith is a private matter. But whatever your faith... it is a fact that when millions of people stop believing in God, enormous public consequences follow. Dostoyevsky reminded us in *The Brothers Karamazov* that "if God does not exist, everything is permissible." We are now seeing "everything."

What can be done? For one, we must once again connect public policies to our deepest beliefs. Right now we say one thing and do another.

- We *say* we want law and order, but we allow violent criminals to return to the streets.

- We *say* we want to stop illegitimacy, but we subsidize behavior that leads to it.

- We *say* we want to discourage teenage sex, but educators across America treat teenagers as if they were young animals in heat, and are more eager to dispense condoms than moral guidance.

- We *say* we want more families to stay together, but we make divorce easier to attain.
- We *say* we want a color-blind society, but we continue to count people by race and skin pigment.

Furthermore, America desperately needs to recover the purpose of education, which is to provide for the intellectual *and* moral education of the young. Plato made the point that good education makes good men, and good men act nobly.

Until a quarter-century or so ago, this time-honored belief virtually went unchallenged. But having departed from it, we are now reaping the whirlwind. We say we desire more civility and responsibility from our children, but many schools refuse to teach right and wrong. And so we talk about "skills facilitation," "self-esteem" and being "comfortable with ourselves."

Most important, we must return religion to its proper place. Religion provides us with moral bearings, and the solution to our chief problem of spiritual impoverishment depends on spiritual renewal. The surrendering of strong beliefs, in our private and public lives, has demoralized society.

Today, much of society ridicules and mocks those who are serious about their faith. America's only respectable form of bigotry is bigotry against religious people. And the only reason for hatred of religion is that it forces us to confront matters many would prefer to ignore....

In our time, we have seen America make enormous gains—a standard of living unimagined fifty years ago, with extraordinary advances in medicine, science, and technology. Life expectancy has increased by more than twenty years in the past seven decades. Opportunity has been extended to those who were once denied it. And, of course, America prevailed in our "long, twilight struggle" against communism.

Today we must carry on a new struggle for the country we love. We must push hard against an age that is pushing hard against us. If we have full employment and greater economic growth—if we have cities of gold and alabaster—but our children have not learned how to walk in goodness, justice, and mercy, then the American experiment, no matter how gilded, will have failed.

Do not surrender. Get mad. Get in the fight.

You know, I will never surrender. And I am mad at what we've allowed Satan to do to our children. That's why I'm fighting harder than ever before to show our youth that in Christ, there's hope.

ONE
An Ordinary Friday on Main Street, USA

1. Rick Bella and Stuart Tomlinson, "Mob of teenagers watches two beat bystander," *The Oregonian*, September 12, 1993, C01.
2. Holly Danks, "Survivor of attack reflects on case," *The Oregonian*, September 20, 1993, A01.
3. Erin Hoover Schraw, "Beating leaves officials frustrated," *The Oregonian*, September 14, 1993, B01.
4. Holly Danks, "Teenagers confess to Lloyd Center beating," *The Oregonian*, September 25, 1993, A01.
5. Ashbel S. Green, "Three held in Lloyd Center beating," *The Oregonian*, September 24, 1993, A01.
6. Compiled from several stories, including Denise McVea, "Portland death spurs question on trauma care," *The Oregonian*, October 7, 1993, A01; "Teen accused in man's death faces trial in adult court," *The Oregonian*, December 3, 1993, D03; and Rick Bella, "Trial begins, renewing pains of Cripps death," *The Oregonian*, April 6, 1994, B01.
7. Rick Bella, "Youth convicted in traffic shooting," *The Oregonian*, April 8, 1994, D01.
8. George Rede and Erin Hoover Schraw, "Lloyd Center beating: bruising a city's psyche," *The Oregonian*, September 19, 1993, A01.
9. Rede and Shaw.
10. "Cities with most increase, decrease in violent-crime rates," *USA Today*, December 5, 1994, 9A.
11. "Cities with most increase...," December 5, 1994.
12. Robert Davis and Sam Vincent Meddis, "Random killings hit a high," *USA Today*, December 5, 1994, 1A.
13. Davis and Meddis.
14. Davis and Meddis.
15. Davis and Meddis.

16. Davis and Meddis, 2A.
17. Davis and Meddis, 2A.
18. U.S. Department of Justice, Federal Bureau of Investigation, *Crime in the United States 1992, Uniform Crime Reports*, October 3, 1993, 13,17.
19. Bill Moyers, "There is so much we can do," *Parade*, January 8, 1995, 5.
20. Moyers.
21. "School violence on the rise in many cities, study says," *Gazette Telegraph*, November 2, 1994, 1.
22. Carol Sowers, "Violence has Utah, Colorado rethinking West's attitude toward guns," *Arizona Republic*, November 5, 1993.

THREE
Where Have All the Families Gone?

1. "Seeds of Trouble," *Houston Chronicle*, August 14, 1994, 9.
2. "Seeds of Trouble," 6.
3. "Seeds of Trouble," 1.
4. "Seeds of Trouble," 2, 3.
5. "Seeds of Trouble," 3.
6. "Seeds of Trouble," 3.
7. "Seeds of Trouble," 3.
8. "Seeds of Trouble," 2.
9. The Arizona Criminal Justice Commission, "Street Gangs in Arizona," 1993, 8, 9.
10. "Seeds of Trouble," 3.
11. Barbara Dafoe Whitehead, "Divorce and Kids: The Evidence Is In," *The Reader's Digest*, July 1993, 122.
12. "Mom urges son to attack neighbor kid," *The Beloit Daily News,* October 15, 1994, 8.

FOUR
R-E-S-P-E-C-T

1. C.S. Lewis, *The Weight of Glory and Other Addresses* (Grand Rapids, Mich.: Eerdmans, 1965), 2.

FIVE
Let's Be Adults about This

1. David Gonzalez, "Bishops battle America's 'culture of violence'" *The Desert Sun*, November 26, 1994, A10.
2. Caleb Rosado, "America the Brutal," *Christianity Today*, August 15, 1994.
3. Rosado.
4. Rosado.
5. Rosado.

SIX
The Victory of Reaching Out

1. Much of this chapter is adapted from Nicky Cruz, *Give Me Back My Dignity* (La Puente, Calif.: Cruz Press, 1993). That book gives a much fuller description of the worldwide work of Victory Outreach Ministries.
2. The *Challenge to Ministry* course is a three-level training program. Level I covers such topics as "Being Teachable," "Contending for the Faith," "Servanthood," and "Stewardship: Learn how to use your time, talents, and money for God's kingdom." "Contending for the Faith" teaches five lifetime values: relationships, discipleship, quality, balanced doctrine, and unity of vision.
3. Here's a partial list of ministries within the church: senior adult ministry; singles ministry; Christian education (children, nursery, Royal Rangers, Missionettes, adult education); evangelism ministry; street rallies ministry; rehabilitation ministry; visitation ministry; pastoral counseling; prayer ministry; music ministry (orchestra, choir, overhead projector crew, sound booth, worship singers); building and grounds and landscaping ministries; vehicle maintenance; administrative ministry (business administration, general office, receptionist, accountant, church bulletins, computer workers); bookstore; silk screen T-shirt guys; newsletter and Sunday bulletin ministry; ushers and security; women's ministry.

EIGHT
Let's Get Our Hands Dirty

1. Kathryn Sosbe, "Teen sentenced to life without parole in slaying," *Gazette Telegraph*, November 22, 1994, A1,A3.
2. Cited in Bill Moyers, "There is so much we can do," *Parade*, January 8, 1995, 6.

3. Cited in "Bang, you're dead!" *The Oregonian*, August 17, 1993, C4

4. Cited in Eugene H. Methvin, "Behind Florida's Tourist Murders," *Reader's Digest*, April 24, 1994, 94.

5. Methvin, 95, 96.

6. Eugene H. Methvin, "We Must Get Tough with Killer Kids," *Reader's Digest*, June 1993, 103-107.

7. Fred Leeson, "Kids and crime: doing more time," *The Oregonian*, October 1, 1993, A01.

8. Jerry Thomas of the *Chicago Tribune*, "Boys Hope offers escape from poverty, crime, despair," *The Oregonian*, December 4, 1994, L12.

9. Moyers.

10. From a newsletter by U.S. Congresswoman Elizabeth Furse (D-Oregon), "Crime Update," June 1994.

11. Moyers.

12. Moyers.

13. Moyers.

14. Lars-Eric Nelson, "Toward a Technological Frisk," *Reader's Digest*, July 1994, 51.

15. "Community Reclamation Project," *Gangs: The Epidemic Sweeping America* (Northville, Mich.: Midwest, 1994).

16. "What Other Communities Are Doing," in *Gangs: The Epidemic Sweeping America*. Information taken from *Breaking Up Is Hard to Do*, National School Safety Center; and *Building Gang Prevention Bridges to Parents and Families*, National Crime Prevention Council.

17. *Gangs: The Epidemic Sweeping America*.

18. Pamphlet from the Arizona Prevention Resource Center, College of Extended Education, Arizona State University, Tempe, Arizona, 85287-1708, (phone) 602-965-9666.

19. Furse.

20. *Gangs: The Epidemic Sweeping America*.

21. From *Youth Gangs: Problem and Response*, the National Youth Gang Suppression and Intervention Program, University of Chicago.

22. *Gangs: The Epidemic Sweeping America*.

23. Tom Hallman, Jr., "'Big brother' helps young gang members turn around lives," *The Oregonian*, December 4, 1994, B1, B8.

NINE
The Future Is in Our Hands

1. David L. McKenna, *The Coming Great Awakening* (Downers Grove, Ill.: InterVarsity Press, 1990), 7-10.

2. Herbert Schlossberg, *Called to Suffer, Called to Triumph* (Portland: Multnomah, 1990), 151-152.

Appendix
The Root of Our Problem

1. William J. Bennett, "What Really Ails America," *The Reader's Digest*, April 1994, 197-202. (Condensed from a speech delivered December 7, 1993, at The Heritage Foundation, Washington, D.C.) Used by author's permission.

SIDEBARS

Where's the Gunfire?

S1. Robert Davis and Sam Vincent Meddis, "Random killings hit a high," *USA Today*, December 5, 1994, 2A.
S2. "Myths about gangs" in *Gangs: The Epidemic Sweeping America* (Northville, Mich.: Midwest, 1994).
S3. "Myths about gangs."

Kids and Violence

S1. Debra J. Saunders, "Crime and violence the real enemies," *Los Angeles Daily News*, May 6, 1992.

A Living Nightmare

S1. Bill Moyers, "There is so much we can do," *Parade*, January 8, 1995, 6.

No Fear of Death

S1. Mark Horowitz, "In Search of Monster," Part 1, *The Atlantic Monthly*, December 1993.

"If I Grow Up..."

S1. Barbara Kantrowitz, "Growing Up Under Fire," *Newsweek*, June 10, 1991, 64.
S2. Kantrowitz.
S3. Kantrowitz.

Life in the War Zone

S1. Brian Duffy, "An American doctor in the schools of hell" *U.S. News and World Report*, January 16, 1989, 32.
S2. Duffy.
S3. Duffy.

The Media Monster

S1. "Gangs: The Problem," in *Gangs: The Epidemic Sweeping America* (Northville, Mich.: Midwest, 1994).
S2. Brad Kava, radio columnist, "L.A. Station Pulls the Plug on Songs with the Wrong Ideas," November 5, 1993, America Online.

What Can We Do about the Media?

S1. Plato, *The Republic* as quoted in Bob DeMoss, Jr., "Giving the Gift of Discernment," *Parental Guidance*, December 15, 1994, 2.
S2. "Parents and Prevention," in *Gangs: The Epidemic Sweeping America*.
S3. *Gangs: The Epidemic Sweeping America*.

Gun-Toting Children

S1. Brian Duffy, "An American doctor in the schools of hell" *U.S. News and World Report*, January 16, 1989, 33.
S2. Duffy, 35.

They're Stealing the Souls of Our Children

S1. Youngster watches as man fatally shot," *Mobile Press-Register*, October 25, 1994, 6-B.

Death in Chicago

S1. Don Terry, New York Times News Service, "Boy's short, tortured life becomes macabre role model," *The Oregonian*, September 9, 1994, A16.
S2. Stephen Braun, LA Times-Washington Post Service, *The Oregonian*, September 3, 1994, A11.
S3. "Our gun-toting young," *The Oregonian*, September 11, 1994, S2.
S4. "Boys, 10 and 11, admit murdering 5-year-old child," *Beloit Daily News*, October 15, 1994, 1.
S5. "Boys admit murdering."

Dead at the Deepest Levels

S1. Charles Krauthammer, "The Scourge of Illegitimacy," *The Reader's Digest*, March 1994, 49.
S2. Krauthammer.
S3. Krauthammer.
S4. Charles Murray, "Tomorrow's Underclass," *The Reader's Digest*, March 1994, 53.

But It Couldn't Happen Here!

S1. "Bang, you're dead!" *The Oregonian*, August 17, 1993, C1. Story based on wire reports.
S2. "Portland homicide logs tell tale of young lives gone terribly wrong," *The Oregonian*, August 17, 1993, C1, C6.

If you would like more information about Nicky Cruz Outreach or the Save Our City invasions, or would like to support us in our work in the inner cities, or receive our newsletter, please contact us at this address:

Nicky Cruz Outreach
P.O. Box 25070
Colorado Springs, CO 80936